"In great Rudy style, Ms. Simone shares her frank honesty and first-hand knowledge of what females on the spectrum need, desire, and deserve. She sheds light on the enigma surrounding females with Asperger's syndrome and shows her readers the whys and wonders behind the female with AS. Thanks to Rudy, I can now see many mutually satisfying relationships possible between Aspergirls and their partners! Right on!"

—*Liane Holliday Willey, author of* Safety
Skills for Asperger Women: How to Save
a Perfectly Good Female Life

"I find this book extremely well written in a language that nonautistic individuals can identify with and get the point of what Rudy Simone is trying to convey."

—*Deborah Lipsky, author of* From Anxiety to
Meltdown *and* Managing Meltdowns

"Rudy Simone does it again! Like her other books, Rudy provides the direct instruction to empower those desiring better understanding and appreciation of women with Asperger's syndrome. The 'Partner's words' ending each chapter succinctly summarize and are great at driving home each one of the 22 points. My highest recommendation for anyone wanting a deeper and more meaningful relationship with the female with Asperger's syndrome in their lives."

—*Stephen M. Shore, EdD, Assistant Professor of Special
Education, Adelphi University, internationally known
consultant and presenter on issues related to the autism spectrum*

"Reading Rudy's second book concerning 22 things was just as enlightening and informative as her first book. Whether you are male or female this book will speak your language. I love the down-to-earth approach Rudy takes and the plain speak she uses to take us there. I love the all rounded, no bull, tackle the unmentionable and answer the hard questions stuff that Rudy refuses to shun. Being in a relationship myself with an Aspergirl I recognise so many of the day to day issues. I wish I had read *22 Things* so many years ago. It would have explained such a lot and saved us from some of the smog. No matter, it's here now. We need this book!"

—*Wendy Lawson, psychologist, qualified counselor, social worker and autism advocate, author of many books on topics relating to autism spectrum disorders*

"In her inimitably warm, witty, and disarming style, Rudy Simone casts light on what you need to know about having a relationship with a woman on the spectrum. One of the most damaging stereotypes of autistic people is that they are uninterested in or incapable of intimacy, and Simone demolishes that stereotype while offering practical, down-to-earth tips that will help you navigate the nuances of forging a lasting relationship with an 'Aspergirl.' Addressing everything from sex, to sensory issues, to emotional vulnerability, to giving and receiving criticism in a caring and safe way, Simone offers a road map that will help you avoid potential pitfalls with the one you love and start building a life of closeness, passion, and honesty together."

—*Steve Silberman, contributing editor of* Wired *magazine and neurodiversity blogger for the Public Library of Science*

22

THINGS

a Woman with
ASPERGER'S SYNDROME
Wants Her Partner
to Know

by the same author

**22 Things a Woman Must Know If She Loves
a Man with Asperger's Syndrome**
Rudy Simone
Foreword by Maxine Aston
ISBN 978 1 84905 803 2
eISBN 978 1 84642 945 3

Aspergirls
Empowering Females with Asperger Syndrome
Rudy Simone
Foreword by Liane Holliday Willey
ISBN 978 1 84905 826 1
eISBN 978 0 85700 289 1

of related interest

The Partner's Guide to Asperger Syndrome
Susan J. Moreno, Marci Wheeler and Kealah Parkinson
Foreword by Tony Attwood
ISBN 978 1 84905 878 0
eISBN 978 0 85700 566 3

Love, Sex and Long-Term Relationships
What People with Asperger Syndrome Really Really Want
Sarah Hendrickx
Foreword by Stephen M. Shore
ISBN 978 1 84310 605 0
eISBN 978 1 84642 764 0

Connecting With Your Asperger Partner
Negotiating the Maze of Intimacy
Louise Weston
Foreword by Tony Attwood
ISBN 978 1 84905 130 9
eISBN 978 0 85700 286 0

Safety Skills for Asperger Women
How to Save a Perfectly Good Female Life
Liane Holliday Willey
Foreword by Tony Attwood
ISBN 978 1 84905 836 0
eISBN 978 0 85700 327 0

Asperger Syndrome and Social Relationships
Adults Speak Out about Asperger Syndrome
Edited by Genevieve Edmonds and Luke Beardon
ISBN 978 1 84310 647 0
eISBN 978 1 84642 777 0

Rudy Simone

22

THINGS

a Woman with
ASPERGER'S SYNDROME
Wants Her Partner
to Know

FOREWORD BY TONY ATTWOOD, PhD
Illustrated by Emma Rios

Jessica Kingsley *Publishers*
London and Philadelphia

First published in 2012
by Jessica Kingsley Publishers
116 Pentonville Road
London N1 9JB, UK
and
400 Market Street, Suite 400
Philadelphia, PA 19106, USA

www.jkp.com

Library of Congress Cataloging in Publication Data
A CIP catalog record for this book is available from the Library of Congress

British Library Cataloguing in Publication Data
A CIP catalogue record for this book is available from the British Library

ISBN 978 1 84905 883 4
eISBN 978 0 85700 586 1

Printed and bound in Great Britain

CONTENTS

Foreword

We know much more about how boys and men express and cope with the characteristics of Asperger's syndrome than we do about girls and women. Boys are usually diagnosed in their early childhood, their features being conspicuous in the classroom and playground, while girls are more likely to be diagnosed in adolescence or adulthood. The reason is that girls have a more constructive way of coping with and camouflaging their social confusion and difference. They can become avid observers of other children and intellectually decipher what to do in social situations; they learn to imitate other girls, adopting a persona and acting like someone who can succeed in social situations; they become social chameleons. Some girls escape into imagination and create an alternative world. They constructively avoid social interactions and playing with other children, choosing instead to engage in creative solitary play, read fiction or spend time with pets and animals.

For the woman who has the characteristics of Asperger's syndrome, there are several pathways to diagnosis, of which you, as her partner, may be aware. She may have been diagnosed as a child or adolescent, in which case she probably benefited from and may still have access to guidance from support services for children and adults with Asperger's syndrome. Another possibility is that she was diagnosed as an adult when the stress, strain and exhaustion of intellectually analyzing social situations, and acting "normal" but being rejected, bullied and teased, resulted in a secondary mood disorder such as depression, or an anxiety or eating disorder. A third possibility is that she had felt different to other children, and had difficulties with friendships and relationships and finding successful employment and promotion and, by acquiring information on Asperger's syndrome, recognized that the characteristics explained her own profile of abilities and experiences throughout childhood. A fourth option is that of a family member being diagnosed with an autism spectrum disorder; the resulting awareness within the family of the range of expressions of autism, including the characteristics of Asperger's syndrome, highlighted that she herself has Asperger's syndrome. This can include her own child being diagnosed with autism, leading to her recognizing the similarities with her own childhood experiences. A final possibility is that, sometime into the relationship, you as her partner started to recognize difficulties in the relationship that could be explained by Asperger's syndrome.

For a relationship to occur and flourish there must be qualities in the woman with Asperger's syndrome (diagnosed or undiagnosed) that are appealing to her partner. There are two types of people who can easily fall in love with someone with the characteristics of Asperger's syndrome. The first are those with a similar profile of abilities, experiences and interests. For example, they both have a great interest in animal welfare and meet as volunteers at an animal refuge; or perhaps they are both librarians, engineers or entomologists. Like attracts like, and both may have similar social, intellectual and relationship needs. The second type are those who are naturally talented in their ability to understand the perspective of others, including the perspective of someone who has Asperger's syndrome. These people may have careers in the caring professions and be gregarious and empathic by nature. These "extreme neurotypicals" can be magnets for those with Asperger's syndrome, who seek someone who understands their motivation and thought processes, can provide guidance in social situations and help moderate emotions.

During their adolescence, some girls with Asperger's syndrome are renowned at school for being extremely well behaved, and are late developers in terms of romantic relationships, having an almost puritanical attitude to intimacy. Their first intimate experiences can be several years later than their peers and their first sexual experiences are with their marriage partners, who may be attracted to their childlike innocence and naivety.

There is an alternative trajectory; adolescent girls with Asperger's syndrome can develop low self-esteem due to being bullied and teased by peers, and rather than enforce social and moral conventions, decide to actively contravene them, becoming vulnerable at a relatively early age to relationship and sexual predators. They may not have the intuitive ability to identify disreputable characters, but tend to set their relationship expectations very low, and often experience multiple abusive relationships.

A small group of women with Asperger's syndrome are notorious for being promiscuous and enjoying sex without emotional attachment; but in general women with Asperger's syndrome are renowned for being loyal and trustworthy, and for having a strong moral code. They may also be admired by their partners due to the positive qualities of Asperger's syndrome they possess, such as their talents in science, arts or languages, or their ability to care for animals, that enhance the attraction for their partner.

The "fall," when falling in love with someone who has the characteristics of Asperger's syndrome, can be to a great depth initially. The relationship is for a while extremely enjoyable, but love is blind, at least to begin with. Over time, various issues can arise that can lead to an awareness of significant differences in both expectations and communication styles within the relationship. The woman's coping strategy of imitation and acting the role of a "culturally typical" woman cannot be maintained indefinitely. Eventually her partner sees behind the mask, and recognizes both the daily challenges faced by someone who has Asperger's syndrome, and the degree of mutual understanding, compromises and guidance that will be needed. This will be a real test of the quality of the relationship.

Within the relationship, communication is often problematic. For someone with Asperger's syndrome, conversation may be primarily to exchange information rather than feelings, and the truth is often more important than compromise or agreement. In addition, people who have Asperger's syndrome often have great difficulty disclosing and expressing their inner thoughts and feelings. They struggle to achieve a concept of an inner self, and have difficulty answering the question "Who am I?" Thus, self-reflection and self-insight to facilitate communication at a deeper level can be elusive. Over time, the typical partner fails to really get to know the inner thoughts and feelings of his or her partner.

We recognize that the emotional repair mechanisms of someone with Asperger's syndrome can be different to those employed by other people, with a greater reliance on emotional repair and emotional safety in solitude. For example, there may be intense enjoyment in time spent engaged in a special interest as a counter balance or thought blocker for negative emotions. The person may choose to spend time with animals to alleviate distress. The typical partner's first choice for emotional repair, however, may be a conversation where feelings are disclosed and shared, or an exchange of gestures and words of affection that act as a soothing and a powerful emotional repair mechanism. For both partners, there will need to be a mutual recognition and acceptance of their different ways of emotionally de-stressing, repairing and recovering.

There can also be differences in the need for social experiences. If both partners have the characteristics of Asperger's syndrome, they may agree on the frequency and duration of social engagements—both wanting to leave a party at the same time, for example. However, while extreme neurotypicals can find socializing energizing and enthralling, the same situation can be boring and exhausting for the person with Asperger's syndrome. When a lack of disclosure of inner thoughts and feelings is combined with a reluctance to socialize with friends, the neurotypical partner can feel lonely.

There are other characteristics of Asperger's syndrome that can affect the relationship. Daily experiences can be affected by the person's sensory sensitivity, especially if she reacts in an extreme way to the adrenalin shock when surprised by a sudden loud noise, for example. Intimacy can be affected by the woman's tactile and olfactory sensitivity; and friendship may be compromised by her being very sensitive to the negative emotional "energy" in a social gathering. She may demonstrate a lack of respect or recognition of conventional social and sexual boundaries, and may not follow society's expectations of femininity—for example, she may prefer to wear practical, comfortable, somewhat "masculine" clothing rather than dressing in a fashionable or feminine way. She may also have an aversion for the tactile and sensory aspects of makeup and perfume.

While we have considerable literature to help couples where a male partner has the characteristics of Asperger's syndrome, this is the first book to describe, explore and provide hope and practical advice for a relationship where a woman has these characteristics. Rudy Simone boldly goes where no author has gone before with insight and enterprise. This book will revive and rescue relationships.

Tony Attwood
Minds & Hearts Clinic
Brisbane, Australia

ACKNOWLEDGEMENTS

I'd like to thank the women and men who generously shared their experiences and thoughts, with transparency and trust: Ann Marie, Audra, Brandy, Brandy, Charlie, Dan, Danielle, Dannye, Donna, Erica, Faye, Fiona, Heather, Hylda, Jennifer, Joanne, Jordan, Karen, Leith, Mike, Natasha, Pam, Sabrina, Sarah, Sean, Sharron, Shyam, Suzanne, Tamora, Tim and Zolf. Forgive those I missed. You all helped me put into words what is often difficult to express, particularly when the need is greatest. I'd also like to give a special nod to Jessica, who has changed my life and the lives of so many others by giving authors a voice.

Introduction

Since my first book *22 Things a Woman Must Know If She Loves a Man with Asperger's Syndrome* (2009) came out, I have received many requests to write a companion piece, about being in a relationship with an Asperger female. The requests were mostly from AS women. Females, whether they have AS or not, tend to want to figure out relationships. Trouble is, AS females are not so good at that. While men seem to be hard-wired to figure *things* out, rather than *people*, my own male partner is much more adept at social relationships than I am. Lucky for me. Not all men are or are even willing to try. This tilts the whole concept of gender roles in relationships on its ear. When you are in a relationship with an Aspergirl, you may need to take the reins socially, and you will need to be sensitive to the special needs inherent in autism. Ignorance is not an option. Denial is not an option—you can't pretend it doesn't exist.

Many people have asked me, "What good is a label?" Why label something Asperger's or autism if the person doesn't seem that affected? The operant word here is "seem." Nobody knows what goes on in a person's interior life moment to moment, and just because they've learned to play ball very well, doesn't mean it's not putting an incredible amount of stress and strain on them emotionally, mentally, and physically. Hence the meltdowns. Anyone who's spent a significant amount of time with an autistic adult or child will have witnessed one. This hurricane of emotion, pain, and fury, is indicative of the amount of turmoil that is going on inside, which is usually brewing beneath the surface. If you love someone with autism or Asperger's, you owe it to yourself to know what things make that storm rise to critical level and what things you both can do to avoid it. Whether it is sensory overload, social difficulties, or cognitive confusion, every problem, every challenge has a solution.

That said, what about the gifts of autism and Asperger's? Finally people are beginning to understand that autism doesn't just mean difficulty expressing emotion, difficulty understanding social cues, body language, etc. It also means that he or she may have gifts. What those gifts are vary from person to person; some may have a mind like a camera or an audio recorder; others have the ability to mimic, sing, paint, write, design, invent, organize, visualize, and more. We're not all geniuses of course, but even if our talents are modest, most of us can focus on our special interests or tasks with an amazing amount of stamina and focus.

So why is this book needed? There isn't a lot of information about female Asperger's, with only a few notable exceptions springing to mind, including Liane Holliday Willey's latest, *Safety Skills for Asperger Women: How to Save a Perfectly Good Female Life* (2011). I've included some more in the resources section at the back of the book. As I talked about in my book *Aspergirls: Empowering Females with Asperger Syndrome* (2010b), Asperger's not only presents differently in females, but is perceived differently because of society's expectations of gender. Within that, each girl, while sharing common spectrum traits, will have a unique profile, personality, and set of abilities. Some of those abilities will be obvious and practical, others may be more obscure and difficult to put to practical use in terms of career or lifestyle, but they are abilities nonetheless. Virtually every spectrum girl will have areas of intense focus and interest, even if those do change abruptly from time to time. How can you, the partner, help those areas flourish so she can create meaning in her life? I've said it many times, and it is my personal motto and belief that "validation and support can mean the difference between a painful existence and a life fully expressed." I know what I'm talking about. I've experienced firsthand the pitfalls of an undiagnosed and unsupported life. Running away from home, being arrested, dropping out of school over and over again, two failed marriages and countless relationships that ended badly, losing custody of my child for a while, wandering the globe like a bedouin with no tribe, being beaten up and otherwise assaulted, statutory rape, poverty, and much much more. As light as this book is, and I've tried to make it as readable as possible, the issues it discusses are serious, and the consequences dire for an innocent heart. And at the bottom of it all, is the innocence and purity that I have seen in every autistic person with rare exception, and that, only because cruelties have tainted it.

I've finally found, in my late forties, the validation of diagnosis and the support of a truly loving and understanding partner. It is the difference between prison and freedom, between happiness and heartache, between heaven and hell to be quite frank. It's not that my life is perfect now and I don't still have meltdowns or struggle with overload on a daily basis. I still go the wrong way when I get out of my car, I still get migraines from flickering fluorescents or sudden loud noises, and even occasionally fall up the down escalator. I still take things literally, even though I'm a comic. I still suffer excruciating shyness and fear of people, despite being on stage. Anxiety is still the basic platform from which I operate. But I know why, and that has made all the difference. That and having someone in my life who says, not only "It's going to be fine," but, "You're fine just the way you are." My hope in writing this book is to help other Asperger females find that kind of love and support. In *Aspergirls*, I spoke directly to the women first and then offered advice to those around them. In this book, I speak directly to the partners.

Lastly, I want to make clear to my gay readers that I include you as well. "Partner" means boyfriend, girlfriend, husband, or wife, and I apologize for any use of gender-specific terminology throughout. This is not intended as a slight, just a convenience. I also think that much of the information will be useful to anyone involved with an Aspergirl, whether a relative, friend, or even coworker.

1

So, you want to date
an Aspergirl?

Let's say that you are not the partner of an Aspergirl, but you've met one that you quite like. Maybe she has told you she has Asperger's, or maybe you've done a little research and you feel fairly convinced that she may be on the spectrum. She at least has a few traits.

You are wondering (a) what's the best way to go about asking her out, and (b) will dating an Aspergirl be as difficult as you may have heard from some sources?

It is going to be perhaps different than other relationships you've had, and will have both rewards and challenges. Apparently, I am told by nonautistic friends (often referred to as neurotypical or NT), there is a courting game, a dance, that men and women do, and they learn it at a young age. Not autistic people or Aspergians, though. Most of us don't even realize there is a game or a dance until we are much older, so no wonder we never learned the steps properly. You are not dealing with a savvy dater. While she may like you and let you know in no uncertain terms, she might not have a clue that you like her. But regardless, I do think it is important to take it slow.

From all the women and men I've spoken with, it seems that the longest-lasting relationships start out as friendships rather than instant attractions, allowing time to build real understanding and trust. They are often based around mutual or at least compatible interests. This goes against the (young) Aspie's tendency to be intensely attracted to things like hair and eyes, which are hardly any indication of actual character or compatibility.

Some happy Aspergirls tell me that their partners seemed to share many of their characteristics, such as being apart from the crowd, eccentric, quiet, gentle. These often turn out to be AS/AS couples, for like often does attract like. Of all my relationships, looking back I can see that many of them were on the spectrum and we sensed a kindred spirit in one another. Of course, if you are NT, you can bring things to the relationship that she does not have within herself, so do not think for a moment that if you aren't on the spectrum you won't relate. And you might have many mutual interests besides.

But whether you are Aspie or NT, the key ingredient here is that you enter into this with open eyes. Her good traits may be great traits, but don't look at the sunlight glistening on the water and tell yourself that it looks calm, because there will be all kinds of things going on under the surface. Even the most self-aware Aspergirls, who face their challenges head on, still have sensory issues, social limits, high intelligence with unexpected cognitive deficits—there are all these things that will challenge you in your ideas of what a woman should be, what she can be and what she is. You may find that the model of your perfect woman you've built in your mind will be quickly torn down and reconstructed. You may get quite upset when this starts happening, but if you are somewhat mentally prepared, you will fare much better.

If you ask her out and she says no, understand that many Aspies have faced a great deal of rejection, adversity, and bullying throughout their lives. As a result, she may be very careful of whom she shares her heart with. My advice is, be friends first and foremost. Even if she is ready to dive into a relationship (as some of us do, whether due to loneliness, excitement at this new suitor, or our own idealism and healthy sexual appetite) proceed with kindness and with caution. Read books, watch documentaries and films on both Asperger's and autism. Asperger's is regarded as being on the autism spectrum, but with its own unique challenges. We may be more present in terms of ability to process and communicate, but because our differences and deficits are invisible, expectations are higher in terms of social understanding and abilities. We have a hard time fitting in to society in general, and we often don't get the support and understanding we need.

If the time is right for a first date, make it clear where you will be going, whether it is dinner or drinks, what people wear in this place, even what the weather will be. It is probably best if you take the reins since she might have enough anxiety to deal with, without also having to choose the setting. Or, give her a couple options to pick from, not a Chinese menu of a hundred choices. And let it be just the two of you, unless you have mutual friends that she would like to invite.

Do not have sex with her (or try to) right away. She is sensitive, and sometimes obsessive, and might not understand if you change your mind after one go, and decide you don't want an intimate relationship after all. Or she might be very put off by premature advances. If you do go out with her and decide that she is not someone you could see yourself having a serious relationship with, tell her and move on. If you are friends, stay friends; but if you are not, make a clean break. Never ever use an Aspergirl for sex. Apparently some NT women are okay having purely sexual relationships. I do not think this is common for Asperger females. Not at all. We like our routines too much to have "casual sex" with different partners on a regular basis. And there would be too many adjustments to make.

If you are the type of person who is overly concerned with what other people think, then you might not do well with an Asperger partner. I once had the perfect boyfriend in every possible way, except for one fatal flaw—he had to keep up with the Joneses, and he hated attracting raised eyebrows.

Sometimes, with an Aspie, that will happen. We don't always do or say what is expected; we can be unconventional, even eccentric. In the eyes of the right person, this is a good trait.

Still here? The rest of this book will be your guidebook in this new adventure. You wouldn't visit any exotic land without one, would you?

PARTNER'S WORDS

"The first thing that caught my eye was her creativity. She had her very own unique sense of style and she didn't really follow whatever was trendy, she just did her own thing. That is one part of her personality that I love, because she isn't concerned with what everyone else is doing."

2

Kit

Try feeling this!

Did you ever read that story called "The Princess and the Pea" when you were a kid? If not I'll fill you in. It's about a girl who was so sensitive, she couldn't sleep because there was a pea under her mattress. They stacked 20 mattresses and 20 feather beds, and she still could feel it. In the story, this proved she was a real princess. In real life, someone like that would not be seen as royalty, but as a royal pain.

Not everyone on the spectrum is this sensitive, but most of us do have a heightened sense or two, if not six. If you've ever spent so much as one day with your Aspergirl, you will know this is true. Sensory issues are the one thing that every partner of an Aspie should be acutely aware of—as quickly as possible. It's a prevalent aspect of AS. Strong smells might give her headaches. Fluorescent or flickering lights might make her feel disoriented. Perhaps she can't touch paper or fold laundry without slathering on hand lotion first. Maybe she only wears soft sweats and t-shirts and still cuts all the tags off. Perhaps she jumps to mute the television the moment those obnoxiously loud commercials come on. Any of this sound familiar?

This is what is known in everyday terms as a high-maintenance girl. She may not even think she's high maintenance, because most of our stuff is about what we *don't* want. This is the good news—we don't generally need bling, or designer bags, or cologne, or highfalutin food. We tend to be natural, down-to-earth chicks. How is that high maintenance? But from an outsider's perspective, sensory issues will at times make her seem difficult or irrational and can affect everything from a trip to the mall to your sex life. They are the underlying factor in a lot of other issues, including social overload.

What causes this? Her ears/eyes/nose/tongue/skin probably look just like everyone else's. If she takes a hearing or vision test, she may test normal. It's the brain, my dears, that magnificent lump of grey matter between our ears which wreaks so much havoc. Our brain, the autistic brain, has its own little set of superhighways that allow certain things to speed along like a Japanese bullet train, while other roads are down for construction or haven't even been built yet. We process differently. Can a loud sound cause physical pain? Yes. Can it kill us? Probably not, but it still hurts. A lot.

Put yourself in our shoes. A cat sitting in front of a television does not see a program—it sees flickering lines only. This is because their eyes process differently. An autistic person senses things differently than a nonautistic. She really isn't kidding, exaggerating, or making it up. I once threw up in a doctor's office because the busy pattern of the wallpaper in the tiny room gave me motion sickness, and I wasn't even ill! Just because you don't experience this, doesn't mean it isn't happening to the Asperger female. Women tend to be more sensitive in these matters anyhow. An autistic female can be the epitome of that.

The brain is a flexible organ, and over time some of these sensory things will lessen in intensity. Food aversions particularly seem to fade with age, and as long as we expose ourselves to new things and to challenges, others will too. Other things might become worse with age, or maybe we just become more self-aware. Then as we get older still, the senses become duller, so that what bothers us at 20 or 40 might not even be noticeable in our golden years. Yay! Something to look forward to!

What happens when too many of our sensory buttons get pushed? We get overloaded, and if we don't catch it in time we blow. Trouble is, we may not even know it's happening ourselves. An autistic infant will have a meltdown in the cereal aisle of the supermarket, but usually the adult will do it in the parking lot, after the stress of concentrating, processing, and keeping it together in a busy, confined space. Transitions are important. When you leave a loud and busy place, and get in the car, if she says she needs the radio off for a while, or the window open, she means it. If she doesn't want to talk for a while and needs total quiet, don't petulantly ask "Why? What's wrong with you? Why's it always got to be about *you*?" Not a good idea. Instead, allow her time to decompress. Of course, compromise is important in any relationship, but during crucial moments it's not always immediately possible. Imagine you've just run a race and you're hot and sweaty and out of breath and someone gets in your face and wants something from you. She may not have run a race but her mind has, and her senses. She needs a few minutes to recoup. After a while, you will be able to close the window, or put your music back on, or whatever it is you need.

Sensory issues can be managed by her and supported by you. Her sensory kitbag might consist of earplugs, headphones, lavender sachet, stress ball, hat, glove, glasses, whatever else she needs to cushion herself from the world (a bottle of tequila is probably not a good idea). You might even try having headphones in the car, so one of you can have music while the other has quiet. A smartphone or portable computer will enable her to pursue her special interests, always a balm for the ruffled Aspie soul.

Like every issue in this book, it's a two-way street. Negotiations need to be done in advance. If you want to hold hands and she doesn't like the feeling, maybe she can bring gloves, for example. You can try to be quieter and she can either wear earplugs or desensitize herself (through therapy or practice). You can both adapt to the sensory issues and meet in the middle, you can live together even when you have different sensory needs, if you have tools and patience, as opposed to a "my way or the highway" attitude—that goes for both of you.

My own partner was a great help to me in the beginning, reminding me to bring my artillery every time we went out. After a while, much of this became second nature, and his support has made me much less self-conscious. As a result, my stress levels have gone down and so has my need for so many sensory defenses. When our needs are met, they take on less significance than when they are not.

There is a definite plus side to this sensory sensitivity—if there was a gas leak in your building, she'd be the first to sniff it out and raise the alarm. She can tell you if you are wearing too much cologne, and in some cases, skin sensitivity can make her very responsive to your slightest touch! That is not a bad thing, once you know how to touch her. We'll talk more about that in another chapter.

PARTNER'S WORDS

"She has a good sense of taste and smell, and can figure out what ingredients are in a dish. If I like something we ate in a restaurant, she can usually reconstruct it."

3

She is not broken...you don't need to fix her

It is amazing to me when I hear women say that they have Asperger's, and one or more of their kids have it, but their husband hasn't read a single book on it, because they "live with it." If that's the case, the relationship/family is not benefiting from the wisdom and experience of others who've been there. It's important to read about, discuss, even attend conferences on autism spectrum conditions (ASCs). While you can pick up quite a lot by osmosis, if you have a prejudice against Asperger's, your defenses will be up and you will notice the negatives a lot more than the positives. You might even be looking at the positives in a negative light.

Your woman will never be cured, and there is no pill that will make it go away. There are medications and holistic concoctions that may help control the anxiety, ways and therapies to modify behavior, but there is no cure for autism. Most of us don't want there to be. While we all want to help reach the children who are isolated and suffering because they cannot communicate, we all know from Temple Grandin's example that with the right teachers and support, not only can even those children be brought into the light, they can *become* one of the lights of this world.

If your girl can understand quantum physics, but can't find the car in the parking lot, are you both focusing on the latter too much? I call this nutty professor syndrome. To the uninitiated it can seem like we're not very smart, yet most people on the spectrum are. In fact, according to experts I have interviewed, we have a higher IQ than the non-spectrum population. But we have challenges too, cognitive deficits. She might have perfect pitch, but not recognize someone she met last week. Maybe she can build a computer from scratch, but will go the wrong way at the corner every time. Do not let these things make you underestimate her intelligence. If your girl is on the spectrum, she probably has special skills, even if she herself doesn't quite know what they are. While we are not all geniuses, sometimes even the most seemingly affected of us can have special gifts. I recently spoke at a conference and I remember one particular young person in the audience who seemed especially challenged. A little later, I saw him playing the grand piano in the lobby, filling the air with beautiful music.

The brain is a flexible organ, learning all the time, but you will never cure her—if you push her to be "normal" you will cause her and your relationship to burn up and out. However, you can help her with her executive function skills. Simply put, the term executive function describes "a set of cognitive abilities that control and regulate other abilities and behaviors" (Encyclopedia of Mental Disorders 2011). For example, she might start a large task like painting a room and be unable to stop for food or sleep until it is done. She may get so caught up in her special interest she forgets to groom and bathe. You are entitled to a partner that can hold up her end of the daily tasks of living, but rather than berate her when she forgets or makes a mistake, the two of you need to sit down and figure out what tools will help with these things, where to get them and how to implement and integrate them into your daily life. There are a plethora of things for assisting executive function, too many to list here, but they can include basic items like calendars, alarm clocks, maps, GPS, to-do lists, scheduled breaks, written instructions—you get the picture. On your days off or out together, if she doesn't have a plan or preference, give three activities to pick from. I talk about cognitive/executive functioning tools in more detail in both *Aspergirls* (Simone 2010a) and *Aspergers on the Job: Must-Have Advice* (Simone 2010b) if you want to read more.

She may get burnout from things that you might not expect—from a dinner party, for example—and there will be days she is exhausted and yes, possibly a little depressed. Sometimes the constant challenges can get us down. And when we get down, we tend to cocoon a bit. I'm a fairly successful person, but I'm still an Aspie. There are days I still lie on the couch watching all three *Lord of the Rings*, still in my pajamas, unkempt hair, eating whatever crap there is in the fridge because I can't face people enough to trawl the single block to the grocery store. There will be times she needs to hole up, rest, and recuperate from the business of life. She may not mind you being there, but then again, she might want privacy while this is happening. Do not take it personally. And please do not judge this need. She'll be back to "normal" in a day or two.

If your girl needs more than a day or two to recover from an upset or social overload, she might be slipping into bad habits or depression. Talk about it. There's always a reason for depression, and one should always look for it before waving the "chemical imbalance" flag. It might be a fixable problem in her life or in your relationship. It may be something as simple as a vitamin issue. I recently read that people on the autism spectrum are potassium deficient as well as having stomach issues (which solved a mystery for me, as every time I had a blood test I was told I was potassium deficient). She might be malnourished. My current partner introduced me to ayurvedic stomach supplements which changed my life. Taking a proactive role rather than a passive or berating one is always the way to go in a loving relationship.

It might be tempting to look at other women and see how capable and social they appear. Do not compare your Aspergirl to NT women! Maybe your coworker is a single mother who manages to put on the suit, the high heels and get little Sammy off to hockey and kung fu class every weekend, talks on the phone incessantly with girlfriends, and has coffee mornings with other moms. Someone like that does not have Asperger's but may have her own issues to contend with. Nobody's perfect.

Until very recently, I still heard people calling it a "disease." It most certainly is not. It is merely a different way of being in the world, and wouldn't be a condition at all, if everyone had it. Those of us on the spectrum realize that we are a minority and need our own "civil rights" movement to bring more awareness into the world. We can adapt, but we can't sand all our square pegs to suit the round holes that the nonautistic majority has created.

If you have been together or even married for a long time, it doesn't necessarily mean that you understand her or that you still don't have a lot to learn about Asperger's. If you had a rare car, you'd probably read the manual at least once, wouldn't you? Obviously this is preaching to the choir because you're reading this, but once you put it down, as the days go by, the info will fade. You might want to keep this manual on your bedside table just as you'd keep that car manual in your glove box, there when you need it.

PARTNER'S WORDS

"It has taken me a while to get used to all the differences and the challenges, but it is so worth it. She is the love of my life, loyal, interesting, smart, and funny."

4

No wire hangers...ever!
Why she has control issues

We've talked about sensory issues. These are part of a larger area of control issues. Your Aspergian darling might take being a "control freak" to a fine art. This is pretty understandable once you realize that anxiety is the platform from which she operates. Control is her way of bringing safety and comfort to an unpredictable, unsafe, uncomfortable world. She is also very particular about what stimuli gets into her brain. Perhaps you have fights about what program to watch on the television, the correct way to fold the towels, the most efficient route to take. Maybe she will literally scream at times if she doesn't get her way. Spoiled brat? No, she came that way, straight out of the box, no assembly required. She needs to know what to expect. Even a Christmas or birthday present she didn't want or expect can make her hyperventilate, angry that you didn't understand what she wanted and that you wasted your money and time needlessly.

"No wire hangers ever!" We all remember the famous line maniacally uttered by the crazed Joan Crawford (played with uber camp by Faye Dunaway) in *Mommie Dearest*. One could wonder if Ms. Crawford might have had Asperger's. I had a similar fit the other day when the clean lines and organized shelves of my closet were decimated by my NT male partner, with hangers at all angles and all over the floor, causing my own decibel level to exceed legal limits. Your Aspergirl might have the same tendency. She likes neatness, or at least organized chaos. Messy lines can make it hard to find stuff, make her dizzy. She probably has difficulty knowing where her body "is" in space—where her limbs start and end and where they are relative to one another (this is called proprioception). So she may at times be the thing that goes bump in the night…and the day.

Sudden changes in either expectations or plan can, and usually do, cause a "software crash" in her head, which can result in meltdowns and confusion, and can exacerbate physical clumsiness and disorientation. One time I landed in an airport and was told to look for a white courtesy phone to call my hotel shuttle. I wandered the large area back and forth several times before finally asking someone where the courtesy phone was. He said "right there" and I turned and finally noticed the glaring sign and gigantic bank of five brown phones (I had taken the man at his word and couldn't imagine them not being white). Afterwards, I was so rattled by the experience I fell up the down escalator. Ah, it's fun to be an Aspergirl.

If she gets in a tailspin over small things, remind her to look at the big picture. Is her whole damn life/house/career a mess, or is it just one moment/shelf/task that went a bit wrong? We can get a bit OCD (obsessive-compulsive), and that can impede life too. Everyone goes back in to check the stove now and then, but if she does it six times every time you go out, that should probably be addressed. The brain is a flexible organ, it grows, it learns, it makes new synaptic connections. Sometimes changing the behavior comes first, and then the brain follows suit. If the two of you can't work this out together, a little CBT (cognitive behavioral therapy) can go a long way.

You can do your part too. If her preferences make sense, for example if she really likes the sponge squeezed out after doing dishes, or the shoes put away on the rack, and you know it will wind her up not to, try to incorporate these small things into your habits. It's not costing you anything, or detracting from you, but adding to the peace and tranquility of your life together. If, after months or years together, you are still doing the little things that annoy her, you really have to ask yourself why.

Rituals and routines are part of this attempt at control and comfort; sometimes they are practical or rational, like coffee in the morning, tea in the afternoon. Maybe they're a bit bizarre, like hugging the same tree goodnight every evening. But whether they are garden variety, or mental safari, woe to those who try and stop her. She needs her rituals and routines (the Aspie's version of R&R), and if they're harmless, do your best to be supportive. However, if she doesn't want to try anything new—new restaurants, new places, new activities—because that means negotiating a whole new set of circumstances, people, environment, flavors, etc. and it's impeding her life or yours, that's a different story. You can encourage her to try new things by going with her, or if it's something you've already done, by providing as much info as possible beforehand, including pics and video. The thing is, once we try things we are as likely to like them as anyone. It is that first step that can be difficult because there will be too many variables we cannot predict. You don't want to get in a rut, so if she refuses to join you, reserve the right to go it alone. If her aversion to new things, or her adherence to R&R is severe, and the two of you can't deal with it on your own, again, CBT would be your best bet.

The need for control can also extend to our own bodies. Some of us might become anorexic as a way to control our changing bodies, or simply to regulate what food we are taking in. Especially when we are teenagers and our parents and school systems and peer pressure tell us what we should or shouldn't do, this might be the one area where a young woman can exert some control. Bulimia means we can eat what we want, or what they force us to, but we don't have to keep it. Eating disorders are dangerous things. Fortunately most women outgrow them in their twenties. This control over our bodies might also be the result of having no control over social situations and not fitting in. Since youth is much more about popularity and appearance than it should be, we might think that if we are skinny enough or pretty enough, we will be like other people and other people will like us. One of the wonderful advantages to having a partner is to have someone to bring us out of our shell, out of our habits and to point out when we are working against our own best interests. Don't be afraid to tell her when she is doing just that. If she didn't care what you had to say, she wouldn't be with you.

PARTNER'S WORDS

"Don't change things too drastically all at once. If there's a change in plan, be sure to verbalize it with her, if not write it down."

5

Everyone's a critic...
but she's better at it than you

I didn't know that being critical was an Aspergirl trait, I thought it was my own special skill, until I heard Tony Attwood talk about females on the spectrum. He said that much more so than our male counterparts, we can be hyper-critical. I'm probably telling you something you already know! This is a manifestation of the Aspie trait of wanting to make things better, if not perfect. On the one hand, it's a very positive trait—we don't make such great accountants, inventors, artists, researchers, scientists, engineers, designers, programmers, and so on, because we are content with mediocrity or the status quo.

Unfortunately, your girl may also turn that sharp attention onto your relationship, and more specifically, onto you. It can be frightening when this happens. You might feel like simple Frodo from the Shire, lost in Mordor, trying to hide from the lidless eye of Sauron, as it mercilessly searches for stray hobbits, or habits, as the case may be. Once she finds one, she thinks she can banish it. But much to her horror, the next day you once again commit the same horrendous faux pas, of slurping your soup, or whatever else makes your Aspergirl burn. Argh!

I mentioned a trait in my first *22 Things* book, about men on the spectrum: how it seems that they may withdraw (physically or emotionally) when they become displeased or disillusioned. I think we girls take it to the other extreme. We put on our deep-sea suits and dive in, yelling "I can fix this!" This might be part of what attracted you to her in the first place. On the one hand, you might think you are in need of improvement. On the other, here is a woman who likes perfection, and she chose YOU! If that isn't a compliment I don't know what is.

If she is taking the time to really look at you and think about you and help you in your personal evolution, you can embrace or reject her efforts. My partner initially balked at my attempts to help his business, but then I said, "Look, I listen to you when it comes to social stuff. When it comes to this, you should listen to me." He got it then. I'm simply trying to help him, I just don't always go about it in the most tactful way. That brings me to an important point—she must be able to listen to *you* in some matters.

Aspie bluntness is famous, or infamous, depending upon who you ask. Why do we do it? To be cruel? Absolutely not. We like to relay information and we like to do it honestly and without games or subtext. Do not assign malicious intent to her words. This will merely gum up the works and cause a fruitless fight. Listen to what she has to say without being sensitive. If she says your breath smells like a scratch-n-sniff episode of *CSI*, it probably does. Take measures to fix it and then calmly point out a better way of making that point in future. Have a discussion with her about this and lay some ground rules instead of defensively blowing up. Post them on the fridge if you need to. Recently I myself posted a reminder on the refrigerator: "Do NOT criticize his cooking, looks, dress, grammar, spelling, punctuation, or anything else!" because I was getting out of control and was constantly on his back, until I just about broke it.

What about praise? You don't hear it enough? Contrary to what you might think, you must be doing really well. I mean, she expects perfection, so if you're behaving "right," why would she say anything? That is the desired norm in her mind. But if she is too quick to criticize and too slow to compliment or feels that her way of doing things is the only way, if, after a while, when, no matter what you do, there's always another level to improve, you might begin to wonder when it is all going to end. It isn't, at least, not without you putting the brakes on and making her aware. You have your own self-esteem to protect and the right to be yourself. You both should discuss putting limits on how much or how often she criticizes you.

Another thing to know? If you are wrong and she's right, she will not pander to your ego and let you win. This is not her ego, it's a drive for righteousness and truth that would make a boy scout leader proud. (She wouldn't want you to patronize *her* and let her win, either.) This is not to say she's always right. In fact, sometimes she'll be wrong, and that might be hard for her to take. Undiagnosed females, especially those that refuse to believe they are on the spectrum, will be more stubborn, because they won't understand what their challenges are, or that they even have any. An undiagnosed person will be more likely to say, "I'm perfect, the rest of the world's nuts."

Diagnosed or not, she herself might be sensitive to criticism. I know I am. This is because we are never quite certain if we are getting social things right, and this will be like telling us we are on the wrong track. Know the "why?" And be as tactful to her as you'd like her to be to you.

I do know there are Aspergirls that have a "live and let live" approach with their partners. As Phil Shwarz of the Asperger's Association of New England famously coined (and everyone has borrowed), "You've met one Aspie, you've met one Aspie." And the same goes for us girls. Yours might be very uncritical, because that is what she wants and needs for herself.

Many of us become stay-at-home moms because we want to raise our child in our own way, but some of us are just hiding in our homes. Those talents she possesses might be better turned outward than onto her family all the time. Support her in her quest for work that utilizes this desire for perfection. Seeing what is "wrong" with a system and knowing how to fix it is an extremely valuable trait in an employee as well as a partner.

PARTNER'S WORDS

"If you've dated mainly NT women in the past, you may have some habits that need to be unlearned. With NT women you have to think of a second layer underneath what they're talking about and thinking, and do a little 'dodge and weave.' An AS woman is merely blunt and there's less tact involved. Don't look for the subtext or the game. It isn't there."

6

Break on through to
the other side

A person on the autism spectrum has been described for years as "being in their own world," and even high-functioning individuals have a hard time "connecting" with others. It's as if we have an invisible shield around us, and this is what I call *the glass wall phenomenon*. It is similar to the "glass ceiling" that women and minorities encounter in their careers, that prevents them rising in the ranks. Affirmative action has been adopted to make this situation more fair, so they can at last get those jobs they are qualified for. Unfortunately, the glass wall around Aspies (male or female) is harder to spot, because for them, it isn't a question of rising, it's a question of staying—in their job, relationship, a room full of people. It's also harder to mandate—how do you protect with laws a social issue that also happens to affect a person's happiness, career, and everything else?

It's impossible to say whether the glass wall is an acquired defense, built up slowly by the Aspie, since we never get adept enough at reading subtext, expression, nonverbal communication, and facial recognition to feel completely comfortable with others, or whether it is a natural part of ASC. I just know it exists for most of us. I talk about it at conferences and see hundreds of heads nodding in recognition. It probably doesn't affect your relationship much, because you are in a privileged position—you see through it. You might have never even noticed it was there. Whether she is holding your hand or opening her heart and home to you, there is something about *you* that has allowed her to feel comfortable doing so. You are special.

Understand that outside of your relationship/family, the glass wall is probably very much intact and affecting most interactions that she has. It's tiring, and yes, it's a little sad. My partner once remarked after meeting two of his friends for cocktails, "It's so interesting to see the way people react to you. I could say the same words as you, but you get raised eyebrows, while I'd get understanding." So few people in my life have remarked upon the glass wall, the way I am sometimes judged or reacted to, that it really did my heart good to hear it. Ignoring what is unpleasant is not going to be helpful. Your Aspergirl needs someone who can honestly observe her challenges, talk about them, understand them, and, if possible, assist in making things better.

You probably know what I'm talking about… Maybe she works in an office and eats lunch at a table alone, or sits outside under a tree. Everyone hangs by the water cooler making chitchat while she just passes by, uninvolved in the conversation. On Friday, the whole gang goes out for margaritas and she doesn't get invited. Or she is never included in playground conversations with other mothers. You know, she doesn't get to play reindeer games. I don't mean to be melodramatic; it is a fact of life for many of us on the spectrum. To look at your girl you see no ostensible difference or reason, yet the glass wall phenomenon prevents a real connection with others *en masse*. I'm not saying she can't and won't connect with *you*, and with others she loves, in a very authentic, deep way, but when it comes to groups of peers, she won't.

It is tempting to blame this all on others and say that they are not being inclusive, and perhaps they aren't. But even if your Aspergirl is invited by the crowd, she might decline an invitation, stating, "I wouldn't like it," or go and eventually find herself in the corner alone. I think this is why so many of us love performing. It is a way for us to connect with, and be liked, if not loved by, the crowd. Not something that happens in social situations for us.

Now, what do you and she do about it? She may seem quite content in her glass bubble. Do you accept it? To a degree, but more importantly I think you have to *challenge* it. A fellow passenger on a plane said to me, after a bit of a stressful situation in which I left my wallet at a security gate and had to hold up the flight while I ran back to get it, "I knew there was something wrong with you, I just couldn't figure out what it was." She was not being unkind, I had gone into pre-meltdown panic mode. I explained to her I had AS. She was glad to have the reason behind the behavior and we had a nice flight together afterward. Whether you and she use disclosure or not, the more she practices socializing, the greater the odds that she will meet others that, like you, see her through that glass wall, or won't even notice it. With more acceptance, she will find more confidence; the glass might even come down completely at times, like a window letting in fresh air. We'll talk about that more in the next chapter on friendships.

I want to add that as an exception to this, I'm hearing from younger spectrum people who are in supportive programs, families, or schools, who don't feel isolated or left out at all. Let's hope that lasts beyond such environments!

PARTNER'S WORDS

"I was completely attracted to her childlike innocence. But not everyone gets that about her. I've tried to explain to her, to 'keep it simple' when meeting new people, not to give too much away, nor expect too much. They can't read her, but she can't read them either. Those things take time. I have to remind her of that, as she is sensitive and she does get hurt."

7

It might seem like her
special interest is herself

For someone who doesn't like to be bombarded with talk, your Aspergirl may pelt you with tidbits about her day from the moment you walk in the door until she runs out of breath 15 minutes later. It may seem to the untrained eye, that this is one self-centered chick. That's not what it is, well not entirely. This is what's known in Asperger's as monologuing, and since you are her partner, you might get the honors of being a one man (or woman) audience. This verbal "minute waltz" happens because she may have been alone and quiet all day, with thoughts racing and racing through her mind without her even realizing it. When you walk in, these percolating thoughts come flying out of her and at you like knives from a carnival performer's hand.

The wrong reaction to this is to scream at her that she's self-centered. She will be utterly hurt, feel completely misunderstood and she'll curl up into a protective ball like a threatened hedgehog. But if you don't want to get pinned to the wall, let her get some stuff off of her chest, then gently tell her at some point, I'd like to speak now, if I may. My partner knows that this ritual is necessary, that I have to clear my head of my own thoughts. But I have learned that it comprises two halves—first me, then him. If I don't follow up with "So honey, how was your day?" I'm not being fair.

Your female Aspie needs to let you talk about things that are important to you and to try and take nominal interest in them. My partner is in the wine business, and although I'd much rather drink wine than hear about it, sometimes I just have to listen. I have my limits though, and when I say "I don't really want to hear about that right now," he knows that I actually mean that I can't. I'm either overloaded, or on my own train of thought and he's throwing debris onto my track.

True conversation is difficult for us, but we can learn that the proper format is not "Enough about me, what do you think of me?" but "Enough about me, what about you?" Still, it's never easy. I get asked all the time how I can get up in front of hundreds of people and speak. Are you kidding me? I'm monologuing, I have a huge captive audience and I'm getting paid for it. It's like I've died and gone to heaven. But the best part is, and this is important, I'm imparting information to people. Your girl, even when she seems to have her own special interest at heart, is usually looking to impart information with the aim of somehow improving a situation or helping other people.

When she does this monologuing, people might get the mistaken impression that she is socially adept and good at chitchat. That is part of the magical illusion of Asperger's. I met a couple in the park yesterday and they mentioned New Zealand, which I know quite well, and I launched into a ten-minute travel guide. Then they mentioned they were looking to move to San Francisco but didn't know which neighborhood, so I became a real-estate adviser. They were very pleased with my input and I could tell that they would never guess in a bazillion years that I had Asperger's, but I know, even if they don't, that should I meet them again, in a social situation, they would be very disappointed in my "standoffish" manner, quiet demeanor, and wandering eyeballs. They'd probably think I'm just stuck up, instead of at a loss for what to say or do. Or worse—I'd pull my goofy nervous laugh, which absolutely convinces people that somehow I must not be the Rudy Simone that writes books, but some slightly daffy impostor.

Actual conversation won't really engage her unless it is something she's interested in, but when she is, look out! Someone might mention her favorite band, film, artist, and off she goes, her tongue sprinting like a racehorse out of the gate. In social situations you can help her, by having a preassigned cue, for when to let others speak. My partner will put a gentle squeeze on my forearm or leg, which works much better than a stiff kick in the shins under the table. She in turn, has to trust that you have her best interests at heart and aren't just being overly cautious or concerned that she's embarrassing you.

PARTNER'S WORDS

"I think she comes across as selfish sometimes. Aspies are only selfish because of self-preservation and purely for survival purposes, not for self-serving reasons. It's much deeper, as opposed to shallow, which is what us NTs have come to understand as selfish. We have to get out of that mindset and come to a point of truly accepting this as a pure reality without our own insecurities getting in the way."

8

She only needs one friend...
and the winner is, you!

As I mentioned in the previous chapter, your Aspergirl probably won't have a lot of friends and might not understand why you need so many. If you are NT, you may have a million friends: from high school, college, your old neighborhood, your sports buddies, your old band days, the time you lived in Boston for a year, and so on. Aspies tend to have one good friend at a time and don't understand how NTs manage to have so many and have a life. I mean, when do you get to pursue your own interests? Even if she's got a thousand online friends, and an AS group she goes to every Saturday, works, goes to class, chances are, in her real-world leisure time, she is a lone wolf. You'll never come home to find her giggling with a gaggle of cosmo-swilling girls watching *Sex and the City*. If she doesn't have you (or another family member) to do things with, chances are she'll go alone or stay home. Why on earth would she want to go to the movies with people? They talk through the good parts and never really seem to get into it the way she does! Why would she want to go shopping with other girls? She'd have to concentrate so hard on what they were talking about that the mission—buying clothes—would be obscured in the haze. She hates smalltalk and often that's what casual friendships consist of. "What restaurants do you go to? What bars do you like? Where do you work?" Who cares?

Eleanor Roosevelt is credited with the saying "Small minds discuss people, average minds discuss events, and great minds discuss ideas." While at times we all fall into each of those categories, it does seem to the AS person that NTs do the former quite a bit more than we are comfortable with. Smalltalk, or talk beyond *our* special interests, can literally sound like white noise to the Aspie. Because she is female, you may have assumptions that she will want to talk shopping, but really she'd rather talk shop. It is all about the exchange of information for her, whether she is an obvious info-geek or not. This doesn't mean she doesn't have friends that she cares about, that she loves. But she isn't going to call them up and say "Let's hang out." Perhaps when she is younger, but as she gets older, the difficulty of dealing with overload, plus loss of the built-in "friend income" of school, university, etc., might mean she'll become more and more used to flying solo.

First of all, explain to her that smalltalk and social scripts are good "gate openers" and can lead to deeper things. They also can take the burden off of deciding what to say. She should know this as a grown woman, right? Not necessarily. Part of the role of the NT in this relationship is to be the social buffer and translator. If you think that is unfair, understand that there will be things she is good at (like math or getting rid of a computer virus), that you are not, and this is what couples do for one another. Lesbian couples will have less of a problem with this, but it is just a little outside the expected "norm" that the man should be the socially adept one, the one with the higher emotional IQ. Chances are, though, an NT man with an AS woman will be.

Though her stamina for work and other things might be exceptional, she won't have the capacity to go out as often or for as long as an NT woman. This leaves you, the partner, in the position of sometimes going out alone, or staying home. Most AS women will be more than alright with your going to parties and seeing friends without her— in reasonable amounts. That amount will vary from couple to couple. If you are often home, she's probably going to be quite happy to have a break from you. That will give her some precious alone time. If, however, you work outside the house at one or more jobs, and have things like the gym and many friends, that is a completely different situation. You'll have to talk about it honestly, as she might not want (or be able) to say "No," but then will resent you if you do leave her too much.

Some AS women say that when they are away from their partner, they lose that "sense of connection" that is a crucial part of our obsessions. When we take an interest in something, we like to have it around. While it is easy to say "that's just insecurity," we all have insecurities. Explain to her that it is quite alright for you to have separate social lives, different friends, and your own activities to pursue, that it does not detract from your feelings for her. Know that she may have been very lonely prior to your relationship. People on the spectrum who are without partners tend to be ALONE, and she may have an aversion to spending time alone because she's been there, done that. Hopefully, you will have similar needs here, as this can become a point of contention otherwise. Every couple will be different and you will have to discuss it. I can tell you that she won't like you springing "I'm going out tonight" at the last minute. Plan ahead. Negotiate. Schedule time for yourself if you need it. But if it's Friday evening and you say "I'm going out with my mates, tonight," you might want to follow up with "And tomorrow, I'm taking you to _____." A positive side of all this is that she will be loyal and (apart from her alone time) she will be there for you—flitting here and there with a multitude of different groups of friends isn't a problem you'll have to contend with.

I think it is also important, healthy, for most couples to do some fun things together, not just in isolation but with others. Especially if this relationship is new, you will no doubt want your old friends to meet your girl and get along with her. Tips: Before you introduce your girl to your friends, you'd best prepare her for them. Explain to her what they are like, who is quiet, who's sarcastic, who will talk her ear off, etc. But I think it might also be wise to prepare your friends for her, especially if she is more obviously affected. This does not necessarily require full disclosure, but perhaps covering what is crucial. You can say things like "She's really brilliant but not good at small talk," or "She is a good listener but has a really hard time with two conversations going on at once," or "She's very blunt, but she's completely honest, not a game player at all." This will predispose them to see these things in a positive light when they come up.

If you do disclose, offer them examples of famous or successful people on the spectrum that they can relate to. Suggest films or documentaries that they can watch, that they'd find entertaining as well as informative. My partner tells everyone (I can't stop him) to watch *Temple Grandin* (the movie). If your friends don't "get" her, you may have to see them on your own. That's okay. If you are both Aspies, this won't need to apply. If you have friends, they must love you for who you are, or they'd soon disappear.

When you are out, never overestimate her capacity for socializing. If she says she needs to go, she needs to go. Other people stimulate the amygdala in her brain, triggering adrenalin and so she has a *fight, flight, or freeze* response to all social contact. This can morph into "performance mode," so if she says she can party all night, take that with a grain of salt, and quit while you, and she, are ahead. The more adept she might seem, the more exhausted she'll be afterward. Do watch out for her. Social overload can happen quickly. The feeling she gets is closely related to sensory overload, but with the added exhaustion of adrenalin burnout. On the way home, for God's sake, do not pick on her in the car, blast music she hates, start an argument, or tease her. After the party, after the commotion, that is when she needs to decompress.

If you really feel that she spends too much time alone, try to get her out and into the community, or encourage her to find others she connects with. It may be that she goes to a class, and learns to dance, but never makes any friends, but there's always that possibility that she will. The more you try, the more likely it will be to happen. Thank heavens for online social networks, which give her a chance to express herself in writing, without the confusing parts—eye contact, reciprocal conversation. Your girl may slowly build up real friendships through this medium, which seems tailor-made for Aspies.

PARTNER'S WORDS

"I need my friends, and she has to understand that my friends are as important to me as her solitude is to her. We thrive on opposite things, but one is not more valid than the other."

HER WORDS

"I love it when I get to be home alone."

"I have a hard time when he tells me he's going out at the last minute because it changes my plans and expectations. I spend most of my time with him so when he goes out without me I usually end up on my own, which is good or bad depending on how I feel."

9

Don't be cruel to a
heart that's true

An Aspergirl doesn't understand cruelty for the sake of it. This is why she makes such a great target for bullies. She is emotionally vulnerable, even if intellectually strong. She is guileless, non-competitive, and doesn't always know when someone does or doesn't have her best interest at heart. This puts you, the partner, in the tough role of being supportive of her dreams and her attempts at interaction, while also watching her back and not insulting her intelligence.

It's a fact—people with Asperger's are often bullied, girls every bit as much as boys. People might think she's weird, rude, naïve, the black sheep, a dozen different things that can cause peckers to peck. This makes it harder for her to go out into the world and pursue her dreams, or career, because she is constantly being blindsided by people that just aren't very nice: "Type A" people who love nothing more than to make others look bad, thinking that will make them look good. They are everywhere, and we, people with Asperger's, don't understand them. If we don't like someone, we will probably just ignore or try to avoid them. We don't play elaborate games to try to one-up those around us. It isn't that we're saints, in fact, in some cases we too become bullies, because we learn by mimicking and because we have pain and frustration and are tired of being the low rung of the ladder, so we may find someone even more vulnerable than us to take that position. But we usually grow out of that as we innately don't like cruelty and there is nothing crueler than berating someone into extreme emotional despair.

I asked my neurotypical partner why he thought people do it. He believes that these bad behaviors are born out of insecurity, and after giving it some thought and observation, I agree. Aspies are insecure also, but we usually take it out on ourselves, not other people. Oh sure, we might snap at our family and partners, but we don't generally muscle our way through the world, trampling on others to get what we want.

Sometimes Svengali-type people come into our lives acting like they want to help us, especially if we are young and pretty, and like trusting wee lambs we let the wolf into our fold. We won't understand they are hoping to get something from us, such as sex or money. We think they love us for our mind or talents, and next thing we know, we are being backed against a wall by some leering character with a long tongue, and it completely catches us by surprise. If we were terribly unsupported and unprotected growing up, we may have been sexually abused or taken advantage of. This can lead to a fear of love or romantic overtures in general, if we never grow a reliable compass for telling good character from bad.

Work too, will suffer if she hasn't found the right job or group to work with. All it takes is one rotten egg to make her shell-shocked. She may not be a good judge of character, but if she tells you that someone is being unkind or if she feels she is being bullied, please don't counter with "Oh, you must have imagined it. They're always nice to me." She's not stupid—she may not know when it started or why, but eventually she will know if she's being bullied. In her mind, that will be like taking the side of the bully and will put a wedge between you. Anyway, why wouldn't they be nice to you? You're not the eccentric behind the glass wall, upsetting people's notions of normal and acceptable.

People are followers, and when someone comes along that is a little unusual, things can go two ways—they will be embraced or rejected. Ambivalence is a balancing act that usually eventually falls to one side or another. You may have friends, lifelong friends, that do not like your partner's quirky ways. They may see the tics, hear the monologuing, witness the control issues, and not know any of the reasons behind her behavior. They may not see the good qualities. Since they probably aren't going to read or research Asperger's, the best prevention here is to praise your girl, talk about her good qualities to others, so that they can see them for themselves. Spotlight her good qualities and utilize the power of positive suggestion.

If her boss, the neighbors, the landlord, or anyone else is picking on her, you may have to step in a bit. For if you don't say anything, and continue to be very friendly, maintaining the status quo with those who are alienating your girl, whether it's at church, school, clubs, neighborhood, then you are being complicit in the type of bullying that is ostracizing and isolating. Even good people can behave badly at times. Someone has to lead the way to inclusion, and in this case what better person than you?

Self-advocacy, especially face to face, is very difficult for us. We might write like Shakespeare, but we're just plain shaky when speaking up for ourselves. She probably gets tongue-tied, angry, or cries. Thank God for typing! Real-time self-defense is not our forte. She has to learn to self-advocate, but it will never be easy or second nature. Even those people on the spectrum who are public speakers and considered "experts" can talk fluently about Asperger's when on a podium, but out of the blue, in a social situation we may stutter and flounder for the most basic concepts to put across.

In case you haven't noticed this yet, your Aspergirl is loyal and hates injustice. You can bet that if ever you were in the position of being bullied, she would advocate for you, and she would stand by your side. She would not take the word of others over yours, or go with the flow. She makes up her own mind about things. This is one of her finest qualities. Loyalty, and a strong dislike for injustice.

And remember, you go home with her at the end of the day, not with your community. If she feels betrayed by you, in a spiritual sense, that will hang over your relationship, and you will never be as close as you could be. While always a kind person, my own partner has really deepened his compassion for those who are different since living with me. He almost seems to prefer the company of those who have some disability, or some flaw or difference that sets them apart somehow. He knows it makes us deeper and a little more compassionate than someone who has always lived on easy street.

PARTNER'S WORDS

"People will show their true colors on this issue, and, fault them or not, you'll realize what their limitations are."

"I *loom*. I've got her back, making sure others get the message. She appreciates the backup as this is something she's never had before."

10

Home is where her
heart is...and her body
much of the time

Aspies are notorious homebodies. It is the one place where we can control all the elements, and where other people do not enter except with our permission. It is an extension of ourselves. Because of our need for a lot of downtime, our homes tend to be filled with objects related to our special interests, whether books, music, DVDs, instruments, tools, and they are often very unique, homey, special places. Even if they are a bit messy, the chaos will be organized (at least in her mind).

What I'd like to talk about in this chapter is how hard it is to get her to leave the house sometimes. Perhaps she has a number of engrossing special interests, mainly things she likes to do from home—such as paint, write, play, research, design. Perhaps she doesn't really like to leave the house to work, seeing it more as a disruption than anything else. This is normal for an Aspie. But just because she doesn't like to leave the house does not mean she is lazy. Of course in this expensive world we live in, most adults need to earn money. Finding work that is rewarding and inspiring enough for us to stick to is worthy of another whole book, and I did write extensively about it in *Asperger's on the Job* (2010a).

But understand she is not indolent, just because her idea of a dream job is one she can do in her pajamas. I love those days/weeks where I have nothing more than a book to work on, for things that I have to get out of the house for on a schedule fill me with dread. Even though many Aspies are great business people, and have many marketable skills, we have to find the right situation, or create it ourselves. The world of ordinary work is often unkind to us, especially undiagnosed, unsupported Aspies. Every time we start a job, it isn't long before people, not the actual tasks, make things complicated. If work was just about work, she'd be fine. But it is a social situation, one that she probably has little control over. She may hate her job, simply because bullies are making what could be a wonderful, or at least tolerable, experience into something extremely unpleasant. If there are mean people or poor conditions at work, every molecule of her body will rail against going there.

Think that she is impractical? That is a concern, but understand that jobs that don't involve her passion will bore her, and hold her interest only briefly. You may have heard her say "I want to be an artist" or some other thing that is difficult to make money at. Should you scoff? No. Never underestimate her ingenuity and fortitude. You probably have witnessed this—when she wants to do something, she usually finds a way...her own way.

Her obsessions may border on the obscure, or impractical. Maybe to you they are just plain weird. It might be anime, it might be insects. She may have the largest selection of clothing tags you'll ever see. She might be able to recite the dialogue of her favorite films by heart. These are things that make her happy. Don't put down her interests by saying she's too obsessive or that they are a waste of time. That's what we do as Aspies. Instead, help her brainstorm ways of turning those avocations into vocations. There are ways of finding out what makes your girl tick and there are ways of putting that to profit. For example, if she is very controlling and keeps lots of lists, imagine what a good office manager she might make. Some of us do love going out to work, and do so happily and successfully, partly because it is some sort of a social life, in a controlled environment where everyone has a role. The trick is to find the right situation. Self-employment, being her own boss, could be another option. In *Aspergers on the Job*, I created something called a Personal Job Map that can really help, and it is something you could help her fill out. It's quite a lot of fun, and if you take your time and do it right and honestly it really works.

Assuming she currently has a partner (you), and especially if you are the primary bread winner, she can use this opportunity to work on turning her special interests into a career. It is often only when the partner leaves, that a woman is forced to find work that is high-paying enough to sustain a family. Presumably you don't want this to happen, but you should still encourage her not to become complacent. Even if you never plan to leave her, you might find yourself made redundant, or something else that could make it necessary for her to earn a living. She should be prepared for that as well as fulfilling her reason for being here. I believe we on the spectrum are given our special interests and obsessions for a reason. We just need to figure out what that reason is.

Even once she does have a fulfilling job and life, there will always be days that she will be a couch potato, that she will have to cocoon. Let's not forget Tony Attwood's advice of one hour of down time for every hour of socializing. If she works with others, that counts as social time. You have to allow her to be a sloth at times, with unkempt hair, stuffing popcorn into a makeup-free face as she sits at computer or watches a film or whatever engrosses her completely and takes her away from thinking about her life for a while. If she doesn't get this downtime, this decompression, all sorts of little unpleasantries can happen, such as insomnia, meltdowns, headaches, depression, and turning you into a newt... Just kidding with that last one.

The world is a very daunting place for an Aspie, and when she's not coping, it isn't that she's being "lazy," or "childish," or "stupid," or she's "turning on the waterworks." She's burnt out; she may not want to be, but she is. That's when she needs something simple, something nice, something to control, and a break from all the effort it takes to get by in the "normal" world. Just because you can cope with it easily, doesn't mean she's the same.

She may also have insomnia as many of us do. It's very difficult to get up and go to work at eight when you wake at three a.m. and can't get back to sleep until seven. In fact, most of this book was written in those wee hours. There are measures one can take to help with that as well, from fresh air and exercise to melatonin, to having more sex and, of course, medication if all else fails.

When it comes to her special interests, they exist for a reason. What that reason is, might not become clear for a while. Disclaimer: It is natural, even productive, for her to be obsessed with information, but not with a person. If she's overly fixated on someone as opposed to something, that is heading into dangerous waters.

She may be idealistic; you will never cure that, but support it wisely with information. If I had known who and what I was, and had support, I'm quite certain that I'd have found more fulfillment and certainly more money than I did, much earlier. I write these books because I came up the hard way and don't want others to have to tread that path. Help her to find a use for those talents that you know she has in a way that makes you both happy. When she is fulfilled as an individual, she'll make a better partner. We need to lean on each other, but if one person is leaning too much, the balance is tipped and it does a disservice to both. That works both ways; while you might love having a stay-at-home woman, if she is seeking greater fulfillment and her rightful place in the world, support it.

PARTNER'S WORDS

"I loved that she wanted to be a stay-at-home mom and that she made our house a home."

11

Even if you think of her as
a woman, she might not

The image one might have of a girl with Asperger's may involve a shy waif clutching a book to her chest; multi-colored hair hovering over a Mac playing games; a porcelain-faced painter sweeping brush over canvas; perhaps you think of sensible shoes, placed under a drafting board or spectacles peering into a microscope; an anime lover or animal lover. But, do you think of power tools? Wrenches, lawn mowers, or flat-pack furniture being single-handedly assembled? Probably not, but she might.

Gender roles and expectations come from societal norms and are imposed upon us. Some sprang from biological differences, but most seem to spring from illogical mindsets. For example, the myth of the superior male driver/bad female driver kept a lot of women in the passenger seat when it is a fact that most accidents are caused by young men. Much of what is expected of both genders is based on outdated social roles—man hunter-gatherer, woman cook and child raiser, etc., and even though that has changed—woman is now every bit as much hunter-gatherer as man is, the moment the plumbing leaks or the car stalls, it is usually the man who leaps to the challenge. Aspergirls buck this trend. If there's a new computer to set up, or bluetooth device, if there's a shipment of furniture from IKEA, if there are weeds to be whacked, she will push you out of the way, and proclaim, "This is my territory dear." And you know this if your relationship is older than a week.

She doesn't understand society's gender roles and may be unwilling or unable to conform to them. She has her own idea of personhood that has nothing to do with mainstream views of females. Even if she attempts to conform to that image, she won't obey traditional female roles or stereotypes for long. I mentioned in *Aspergirls* that fathers might overlook this trait in their bookish, shy daughter, but hopefully as she has gotten older, this trait has ripened. Disclaimer:

Some of us have certain coordination issues that do make operating heavy machinery (or even scissors in my own case) hazardous, but I think it's safe to say we are gender-benders, at least in our own mind.

This plays out in a relationship in a few ways. Early on in the courting stage, she may have been the one to ask you out. She may have pursued you, or even called you a little too much. But it took the pressure off of you to do the work, didn't it? Sometimes things that we like about someone in the beginning, begin to grate on us after a while. She might take the reins too often in bed, in conversation, in the types of things you do with your day. This is not because she is a pushy, aggressive personality. It is that she is a person, not a woman, in her mind. I mention in the chapter on sex (Chapter 13) that this can be challenging for the male partner, as it may challenge his own idea of masculinity. He must be secure in his own self, and comfortable with a woman who has no problem disagreeing with him, who challenges his arguments, who is as cerebral as she is emotional (if not more so), so that this doesn't cause problems for them both sexually and in every other way.

She may not let her own cherished interests and career goals take a back seat to yours. These are the fuel which drives her engine, and without them, she might break down and rust away like an old car. She can become highly depressed and largely inert without being able to act on her obsessions. That is why it is important that information and activities are her obsession, and not other people, who may have agendas of their own that don't involve her. This is also why, as I mentioned in the last chapter, you need to make sure she isn't a stay-at-home wife or mother because she's hiding from the world, but rather because that is where she really belongs at the moment.

Once again I want to make clear, that I do not mean she should get her way all the time, and you should be reduced to wearing high heels and apron while holding the baby on your hip (although if you want to, she'd probably be okay with that). I mean that your relationship is your relationship, not society's, not your parents', or your friends', or anyone else's. It's a clean slate, to make of it what you will. You might think that this doesn't apply to your girl, but if she is on the spectrum, and she is very feminine in appearance and demeanor, then she has either mimicked to the point of genius, or she has actually taken that on as a special interest. Even the most outwardly feminine of us, will still be gender-benders on the inside. I've spoken to many straight Asperger women who had phases of living as a lesbian, or bisexual, or even transgender, for long periods of time, until they figured out it wasn't quite what was needed for them, and that they just needed to express their more male side, unfettered, for a while. One of the reasons we probably won't have many NT female friends, is that we believe that NT females are competitive, where we are not, in terms of wanting to be higher in the pecking order, getting male attention, etc. We tend to be (like male Aspies) more comfortable with the opposite sex because of this, as well as with people not of our own age group.

PARTNER'S WORDS

"I liked her because she was intelligent, hard-working, good with finances and not chuckle-headed like so many other women I'd met."

12

Her name isn't Mommy...
no matter how much
she loves her child

As I mentioned in the last chapter, while she probably won't ever be content being known as "so-and-so's girlfriend or wife," even being "so-and-so's mother" might be an insult to her intelligence. Why must we take the back seat to our loved ones? It seems to us that male partners and children get to keep their identity while ours is sublimated. Being someone's mother is a loaded condition, a loaded statement. Don't think so? Think about it. The moment you hear the word mother, you immediately have a whole universe of iconic images and connotations in your mind, from Carol in *The Brady Bunch* to Stan's mom in *South Park*. But whatever or whomever you picture, there is probably a certain amount of nurturing involved, as well as images of home and hearth. Did we ask for this? No. We might picture ourselves more like mother lions than mother hens. Does this mean we are bad mothers? Absolutely not—we can be fiercely protective, creative, communicative, just not conventional. Egads! Who would want to be?

My daughter has never been known (except by way of initial introduction) as Rudy Simone's daughter. I, on the other hand, have been incessantly called Lena's mother, more times than I could possibly recount, by teachers, other parents, myself as a point of reference, and by my daughter herself. Don't get me wrong. I love being her mother. She is a gorgeous human being in every way imaginable. But as an Aspergirl, I rail against assumptions of both gender and motherhood, and norms that I think are disrespectful and illogical, which, at their core, were created to keep good women down. Of course, it seems that millions of hockey moms disagree with me.

If you have children with your Aspergirl, you may have assumptions about how moms are supposed to behave, and the inherent "mom gene" we are supposed to have. Well, guess what? We might have as much of that as you yourself do. She might secretly find the screaming, pooping infant fairly "useless" in the beginning and won't get excited about parenting until the baby is able to interact in a more interesting way. Even then, when the kids fall down and scrape their knee, you may have taken on the role of nurse, cleaning the cut, administering the band-aids, comfort, and cuddles. That would not be abnormal for the partner of an Aspergirl. Does this make her a bad mother? No. She might have taken on a more traditionally fatherly role, helping with homework, creating projects for kids to do on weekends.

When I interviewed Aspergirls for the book of the same name, I found that sensory issues can make baby-raising difficult, whether it is due to incessant crying and screaming, pooping and vomiting, or other issues, like taking over all the time we used to devote to our interests or just chilling out. And an Aspergirl will not mince words or sentimentalize the situation. Puke is puke and it ain't cute. She probably needs a lot of downtime from tantrums, noises, kids' television programs, friends coming over, fights between siblings— more than a non-spectrum mother would. But what we have in spades is an awareness of our children as individuals, as thinking, sentient beings, much more than ego-gratifying extensions of ourselves. And in the end, we will love them as much as you and as much as an NT mother, we just show it in our own way.

Your kids might come to her with social issues and she throws up her hands, at a loss for what to say because she knows they are more socially aware than she is, if they are NT. She might also talk to your children like they are a bit older than they are. I've noticed that we are not extremely age conscious. She probably never talks baby talk to your babies, although she is quite happy to get down on the floor and play with them. She might be disgusted by changing diapers, but is much more matter-of-fact when discussing sex and other real issues.

Your partner will also be super-aware of bullying and other issues, and emotional well-being will probably be something she monitors vigilantly, having been bullied and isolated herself. Yes, she may have embarrassed your kids or you once or twice; yes, she may have had meltdowns in a superstore while the kids looked on red-faced and helpless. I don't excuse it, but it happens. I have had meltdowns in front of my daughter that I'm not proud of, but I'm on the autism spectrum and sometimes—less and less as I gather more and more tools and support—this happens. They spring up almost out of nowhere. Having an unusual mother makes for unusual kids, and by that I mean extraordinary kids. Kids with compassion, children who don't necessarily have to go with the flow. Innovative thinkers.

She will be an unconventional mother, who will be very hands-on. She may even want to overlap her obsessions with her child's interest, for example, I taught my daughter singing, which suited us both. One artist mother of an Aspergian boy said her son was obsessed with elevators and she with painting, so she took him with her to paint elevators! She might be hands-on to the point of home schooling, or wanting to spend more time at home, seeing that raising her kids is more important than keeping up with the Joneses. Other people may see that as lazy, old-fashioned. Let them. If she's capable enough, and it's the best option, why not? Others are happy being the breadwinner while Daddy is the stay-at-home parent.

She may need you to help with things like sleepovers, even kids coming over. Kids are messy and noisy, and young teens especially seem to listen to music which is about as appealing to an adult as fluffernutter. Younger kids are much more under our control. We pick out what they wear, what they eat, what they do, but as kids get older and we lose control it can get a little tougher. It is to be hoped that she will understand logically that this is how nature works—kids slowly distance themselves from their parents so that someday they can fly the nest. And don't forget that the transition, once they do fly the nest, will be very difficult for her, as it means change in the household, the routine, and her kids may be the only friends she has besides you. She needs to be able to allow her kids to go off to pursue their lives without worrying about Mom.

Your role as father has to be respected too. While you may have taken on some roles or duties that a male stereotype may balk at, who cares? What matters is that you and your Aspergian partner are creating your own dance, and not working at cross-purposes with each other. You have to cast aside any fantasies about perfect mothers, or what you know from your own mom. If your mom was a great one, then what's to stop you incorporating her traits into your own parenting skills, rather than trying to get your wife/partner to do it?

My father made my mother spend all her time learning to cook like his mom, who had, in turn, learned to cook like her husband's mom. Yes, my mother made a mean pie crust, but frankly, I'd rather she spent more time talking to me about what I'd learned from the encyclopedia section I'd just read. And your kids might feel the same way, particularly if they too are on the spectrum.

I wrote in *Aspergirls* about finding an NT friend to give advice on things when needed, whether it has to do with the prom, or friendships, or any other area where your Aspergirl mother might flounder. Although this is particularly pertinent where single moms are concerned, it couldn't hurt here either. But, if you have a mom, friend, sister, etc. who puts their two cents in on raising your kids, they'll preferably know and understand what AS is, and must respect your partner, or you will have a mess on your hands.

Does having an Asperger partner mean you'll have Aspie kids? Maybe. Autism is caused by genetic *and* environmental factors, this we know, although exactly what those factors are is unclear. Unlike some so-called autistic organizations that claim to "Speak" for us, most people on the spectrum would not change who they are, they just want more understanding. Never forget that autism often carries with it some narrow but deep interest(s), and special skills that can change the world. As Temple Grandin has famously said, "Take away my autism, you take away my genius." So if you do have a child or two on the spectrum, you have an incredible opportunity on your hands to help those children reach their own potential, level of self-acceptance, and personal satisfaction.

PARTNER'S WORDS

"She's very responsible as a mom, always looking out for her daughter's best interest. She is authoritative, but there's no manipulation in it—she doesn't let her own feelings get involved in decision-making, other than being motivated by love."

13

How to turn a hotbed
into a hot bed

Your bed may be hot, or it may just be a hotbed, as sex involves communication, sensory, and gender role issues. It can be hard to let yourself go when there are so many things going on—smells, textures, sounds, feelings both physical and emotional. Your Aspergirl may be sexually voracious, she might detest it, or she might vacillate between the two. One thing I don't hear too much of, is a blasé attitude towards the act. She's probably a bit complex in bed to say the least.

For her, sensory issues might make sex something more akin to being strapped into a dentist's chair, and being poked and prodded, inducing panic, fear, and dread, rather than pleasure. While for you, it might be a minefield of self-esteem bombs. As in everything else, there isn't too much tact or game-playing involved. You might be in the throes of passion, when she suddenly tells you to get up and go wash because you smell funny. If she tells you it hurts when you touch her in a certain way or a certain place, believe it and try a different tack. If she's very sensitive, certain areas like the clitoris or nipples might be a no-fly zone. Some girls are so sensitive on the surface, you can skip foreplay and get right to the nitty gritty. She might be less sensitive and need intense stimulation. Whatever the case, it can be deflating when you are trying to warm up and she's giving directions like a traffic cop.

Black and white thinking might make her assume that all sex is the same, so if she's had bad sex, with the wrong people, she might be loth to try again. She might be worried that she's with the wrong partner. She may be unable to ask for what she wants, because she may freeze or shut down during the act. This brings up an important point, especially for younger women. She might not want to have sex, but be unable to say no because of that temporary shutdown, confusion, conformity to peer pressure. You need to have her verbal consent to have sex with her, especially if she's prone to this sort of thing. I am an older, high-functioning, more experienced gal, and I can show my partner nonverbal consent, but when I was younger? No, absolutely not. This is why my first experience was statutory rape in the front seat of a car.

Extreme sensitivity might mean that she wants sex all the time…or never. I have heard from many young women that while their senses overload during sex, they're not actually very sensitive "down there" and so at best, merely tolerate sex, and at worst, detest it. I've also talked to women who were that way with one man, but quite enjoyed sex with another, who "ticked all the right boxes."

Your Aspergirl is as self-taught at sex as everything else, meaning, she didn't have the circle of girlfriends to tell her what to expect, and she was probably too shy or clueless to try and find out. Early romantic relationships might have been all in her head, involving her and a fictitious character, pop star or actor, while in real life we gave it away to anyone who wanted us, because very few did. On the other hand, some girls I've spoken to, who are well into their twenties, cannot let themselves go enough even to try it once. We can also confuse sexual desire with love, and assume that because we make a man sexually satisfied, he'll love us forever, and we can be quite shocked and confused when we never hear from him again. We can be very old-fashioned, conservative, and literal if all we know about marriage, sex, and courting is from a 19th-century novelist. For many years, I thought that sex was just two people lying next to each other naked. I was shocked when I found out, quite a bit later than my peers, that to be a female in the sex act meant you were a "receiver of swollen goods." There needs to be more graphic information directed at young Aspergians to educate them on the science and biology of sex, as well as the potential pregnancies and diseases as well as the ethical side of it.

Without getting religious, there is a moral side of it, e.g. not letting a married man seduce you. Shana Nichols' book *Girls Growing up on the Spectrum* (2009) delves into AS girls and sex deeper than most, and *Making Sense of Sex* by Sarah Attwood (2008) is also excellent.

We can also be pragmatic and see sex as currency; young vulnerable girls on the spectrum could be tricked into formal prostitution or exchanging sex for food, money, or other commodities. I have heard stories of Aspergirls wanting to be paid, by their partners, for sex. This needs to be immediately discussed, and it needs to be made clear that is not an acceptable situation. It is just her connecting what seems to be at the time, logical dots. A bit of compassion, education, and hindsight and she will see the error of this.

She may have had a bad start in the world of sex, possibly masturbating at the wrong time or place, or she may have had little idea of how to go about dating, being unaware and inept at playing those gender-role games that NT boys and girls play, that dance that they do. She may have asked boys out and been ridiculed. She may have stalked or obsessed over one (or many) and gotten in trouble for it.

She may have been told sex was "bad" to keep her from doing it as a youngster and might be unable to break free from that easily. Sex might make her feel objectified, like a porn star, and conversely, she might appear to be using you as she goes about the business of her own orgasm, unaware of your needs in bed, physical and emotional. All of these things need to be handled with discussion and information. Sometimes just verbalizing our needs, explaining our fears and realizing that our partner "gets it," is all that is needed.

There may also be an issue of her appearance—if you are a man you are a visual creature, and probably require some sort of visual stimulation to intrigue you. While she probably shines up as well as or better than most in your eyes, I think it's safe to assume she's not exactly Paris Hilton in the grooming department, nor would she want to be. You might have found her constantly messy, unprocessed hair, sweat pants and t-shirt cute in the beginning, but no more. She lacks theory of mind—she doesn't need to see you in sexy lingerie, so why do you need to see her in it? By the same token, even though she may not have great self-image, she tends to take a more rational view in bed: "If a partner's interested enough in me to sleep with me, then I don't imagine that he's secretly performing a detailed critique of my body during the act." Try explaining that your needs are valid and you'd hate for something so small, such as a hairbrush or bit of lipstick to keep you from hitting the happy zone.

You might find that she loves sex because it is the one time and place that she really connects with another person. Emotional and social intimacy, which may have been lacking all her life, now is offered in the form of sexual intimacy, and can be quite addictive. This can cause an Aspergirl to misread another's intentions, allow her to be misused. If you are her partner and she wants sex too much (believe it or not, this can happen), this might be the case. Take some of those opportunities to work on connecting emotionally and romantically instead.

She might love staring into your baby blues (or browns, or hazels) in bed or out, but don't take it personally if she doesn't, or think she has something to hide. Avoiding eye contact is a very common Aspie trait. Eyes contain too much information and eye contact can feel invasive, if not painful. And if she doesn't want to be touched on a particular day or moment, don't assume you've done something wrong, ask if she is feeling overloaded.

So, what is the key to unlocking the passion of the Aspergirl? Don't push her sensory buttons (in a bad way) and do make her feel safe. If she's on high alert, expecting to be scratched, chafed, bombarded with unpleasant sensations, she'll be as excited to have sex with you as she would be to get a tooth filled. I think the risk here is that you, the partner, might assume that since she's fairly fussy all the time, that it isn't something you can do anything about, so you need not bother trying. This is not something you can brush aside, for a good sexual relationship is crucial to a good romantic relationship in most cases.

Communicate—before, during and after. To be with an Aspie requires emotional honesty and integrity. She might pick up on whatever you're feeling, even if you're not aware of it yourself. Learn what you're feeling, what you need, and how to talk about it honestly. She'll appreciate that, much more than guessing. Soon sex will be something to be enjoyed, rather than avoided or endured.

PARTNER'S WORDS

"When NTs are dating, sometimes we're not really looking to emotionally connect, we're just looking to get laid, but with a female Aspie there has to be an emotional connection otherwise it's a scary situation for her. There needs to be as much communication as possible."

"I'm an openly affectionate person, so my initial urge (no matter my current physical location) is to act upon that. With an Aspie girlfriend, I've curbed that considerably. As long as I communicate to my partner what I'm feeling at the time and ask, most importantly, if it's okay to show my affection, all is understood and clear."

14

Why soothing behaviors
(formerly known as stimming)
are good for her...and you

Everyone has a soothing behavior that they are barely conscious of, whether it's drumming your fingers on a table top, or bouncing your leg up and down in the cinema; we all do them. It doesn't mean you have Asperger's, but you probably can relate to this trait. Because anxiety is our primary emotion, it's helpful for her to let off steam in this way, rather than keep that feeling locked inside. You wouldn't want the proverbial kettle to blow.

Your girl might rock while sitting or sway back and forth on her heels while standing, hum, finger flick, hand flap, twirl her hair around her finger, or a million other little things. Why? Because it feels good. Soothing behaviors at this level are harmless. I think the phrase "self-stimulating behaviors," or "stims" as they have been called, is a misnomer. Although we might sometimes do them when we're bored to keep awake, we mainly do them when we're anxious and need to soothe that feeling.

But if you repress them, they can morph into something else a bit more sinister. As an example, I used to make a clicking sound in my throat when I was a kid because I was nervous around other kids and too physically and emotionally repressed to do anything that required visible movement. I thought no one could hear it, like I had my "cloak of inaudibility" around me or something. Oh, they heard it alright. When my "friend" finally pointed it out to me (in a not very nice way) I was so embarrassed and horrified that I started doing other things, quieter things. First I started biting my nails, ripping off my toenails, sucking on my hair, chewing it, picking at my scalp. Then I developed eating disorders, anorexia and bulimia; things that chipped away at me, made me smaller, as if I wanted to be invisible or not exist. Perhaps if I had rocked instead, or found some other outlet, I would not have developed these self-destructive habits. "Replace don't Repress" should be the motto here—for children and adults alike.

If you are at a public event, say a dinner party and your girl's hands start to curl under until the backs of her wrists are white, she starts rocking back and forth, fidgets with her hair, looks generally miserable, what do you do? Even before that, what do you think? Do you feel embarassed for yourself, or concerned about her? You and your girl should have an agreed-upon strategy if she starts to feel so anxious that she begins to engage in soothing behaviors in public. While a little bit of rocking is no big deal, my boyfriend knows the signs of anxiety and if he's not too wrapped up in a conversation to notice, he'll place a gentle hand on my leg and say quietly, "You okay?" Usually that's enough to reassure me that I'm not alone and I can relax. If I'm not able to answer, he'll take me aside somehow and ask me what I need and act accordingly, even if that means taking me home. If he really needs to stay and I really need to go, he'll arrange for a taxi. I try to be the kind of girlfriend he can bring along on any outing, but frankly, sometimes I just can't. Sometimes it's better to say home than inconvenience your partner or make a minor scene.

Your girlfriend, if in a similar situation, can go to the ladies' room, or go for a walk, excuse herself for a while. But the best cure for this, is to surround yourself with people who do get it. Last time I went to lunch with a bunch of really conservative people, I felt very anxious. I told them I was on the autism spectrum and that I sometimes needed to rock or do this (demonstrated my finger flicking). It went in one ear and out the bloody other. "Oh, you don't have to be nervous around *us*," they said. The moment I hear those words, my anxiety jumps through the roof because I know they don't get it. I wanted to ask "Why, aren't you human?" but I was nice and I didn't.

Outings where the main activity is chitchat will be more difficult—dancing is publicly sanctioned soothing behavior, and so is rocking if you are watching live music. Skating, swimming, biking, any exercise will release anxiety and will be much more comfortable for her than sitting and talking (unless of course, it's about her special interests). Of course, not all stims are born out of big anxiety; often, little displays are reactions to little stressors. But little stressors can become big ones if you say things like, "What the hell's wrong with you? Are you retarded or something?" Believe it or not, many of us have heard these types of comments, from our parents to our own partners.

I spoke at a school campus recently that had a whole room full of sensory toys to soothe and excite autistic kids. I didn't want to leave it. All schools should have one. But your girl's an adult. Maybe you can create a room in your home, where she has these types of things, from nature sounds to bouncy balls to things you can wrap up in. Pilates balls are great for bouncing, and stress balls and soft furry things that she can touch for comfort (she can take these out and about) are good too. Plenty of exercise will help strengthen her nervous system, as will holistic remedies, unconditional love, and of course, the pharmacists' favorite, medications. As usual, meds should be the last resort. Do be proactive in helping set up your home to have a sensory room or corner, and do have agreements and cues for when you are out and about and she is getting overloaded. Stick to it until it becomes second nature. When you are someone's partner you can't take what you need of their love, their beauty, their intelligence, their help, and then when it comes to their struggles say, "Oh go sort that out, will you?"

PARTNER'S WORDS

"After being with an Aspie for two years I find myself rocking and twiddling my fingers in the air...and not to the sound of my favorite rock tune—it's contagious and comforting. Do NOT try to deter or stop your gal in mid-soothe, you will regret it. Join in or just allow her to follow through with her process."

15

Jumping for joy...
or bouncing, or twirling

I have seen Aspergirls young and old, but especially young, who are incredibly stoic, their faces just don't show much emotion. People on the autism spectrum have naturally lower muscle tone that NTs. (I think the low muscle tone contributes to a youthful appearance—it takes years before we get those rubbery, expressive faces that others have, and so we probably don't wrinkle as early as NTs.) But the other reason for stoicism, is that many of us have been made fun of, by parents, teachers, peers, and siblings, for expressing joy and happiness in our own exuberant, uncool way. That can make us repress feelings of happiness.

It is to be hoped that your Aspergirl, presuming that she's at least old enough to be in college or older, has come to that wonderful age of self-acceptance where she lets herself express glee in a natural way. Those ways for us include pretty much everything you'd see a small child do. Laughing, clapping, making high squealy noises, giggling, jumping up and down, snorting, rolling around on the floor, even breaking into a happy booty dance. Ah, yes, we are a sophisticated bunch. This from a load of women whose average IQs are higher than well, yours, if you're an NT. Sorry, but it's true.

She has behaviors that border on the juvenile, and weird. This is another reason we can make such good mothers. We can get right down with the kiddies when *Chitty Chitty Bang Bang* comes on and sing all the songs, then go to work and design rockets. This reminds me. This is another reason she possibly hates going to work. Everybody has to act so damn grown up! What a crashing bore. I once had dinner with Temple Grandin. We talked about *Star Trek*, the Beatles, and *The Lone Ranger*. There was a lot of giggling. All the stiff shirts were down the other end of the table, looking very Serious. The day my gold medal for *Aspergirls* arrived in the mail,

I got so excited, I couldn't calm down. So did I celebrate with a load of sophisticated friends over champagne and caviar? No, I spent the entire evening bouncing on a ball, watching and singing along to *The Sound of Music*. I'm 47 years old. Did my partner think it odd? No, he loved it.

Some of the things we do to express joy are similar to our soothing behaviors, because our emotional cup is running over and our bodies simply cannot contain it—she might finger flick, flap her hands and rock when she's excited, but you'll know the difference by her expression, words, or laughter. She might want to dance, twirl, recite, hum, skip. She might hop on a trampoline, play kids' games (with or without kids), laugh and squeal with delight. Her giddy moments are few, rare, and treasured. She'll get enough odd looks at the playground from other mothers, when she's climbing on the monkey bars with your three-year-old, squealing and giggling. Does she get them from you?

Do you think your girl is immature, or an absolute delight? Do you smile and tell her she's cute and that she should never change, or do you scowl and say, "When are you gonna grow up?" I hope you get excited for her, perhaps even join in her joy. If you want to squelch her happiness, she really won't want you around for long.

These excitement behaviors might be okay to you in private, but if your friends witness them, how do you handle it? I've been called childish and immature when people have seen some of my little happiness outbursts. It hurts my feelings and makes me scowl. It also makes me feel sorry for the person who said it because they have lost the ability to play like I have. But I have learned, and most grown Aspergirls will learn too, when not to reveal too much of this inner child. It's not like you'll be at the company Christmas party and she'll run downstairs with the boss's kid's dinosaur collection growling at everyone. She'll wait till she's alone or at home before she goes full-tilt boogie. It's just harmless fun. If someone insults her, stick up for her and say, "She's just happy."

This is the other part of my theory as to why Aspergians seem a bit young for their age: "neoteny," which has been associated with autism, is the retention of juvenile traits that results in keeping youthful physical characteristics. To be young at heart is to be young of mind, which in turn should lead to more brain plasticity, openmindedness, and willingness to learn, despite our rigidity. Ah, we can be such contradictions. That's what makes Asperger's so damn interesting!

Some women are perhaps a little too reluctant to grow up. If your girl is 25 and she looks and dresses like she is 13, that has social and sexual connotations that could cause problems. I'm talking about harmless fun, not delving into dodgy or risky areas. If you really feel she is jeopardizing her reputation and safety, then yes you should make these points known, clearly, privately, and with compassion. And of course she should deal with adult tasks, such as balancing the budget, dealing with her kids' problems at school, earning an income, all the things a grown-up needs to do. She may be quite proficient in these areas, but if not, they can be addressed one at a time. She does need to learn to stand on her own two feet as much as possible.

PARTNER'S WORDS

"I like when she's playful. Her heart feels very much childlike and a woman's at the same time, which I find to be rewarding. I don't see anything wrong with it."

16

Tongue-tied but not twisted...
just because she can't verbalize
her emotions, doesn't mean
she doesn't have them

Even the most stoic Aspies have emotions, they just don't process them in the same way or time that you, an NT, might expect. Does your Aspergirl have compassion and empathy for others? Without splitting hairs on the difference between the words (which changes depending on which dictionary you consult), I think that Aspies are some of the most compassionate people there are, when it comes to real crisis, real pain. We'll rescue injured animals, help old ladies open doors, and rail against social injustice. We create and improve systems all the time, to make things better, not just for ourselves but for others, whether on a small scale or global.

But in ordinary, day-to-day circumstances, we can seem quite the opposite—cold and unsympathetic. If someone tells your Aspergirl that their $200 shoes broke a heel after one wear, she might say something like, "It's stupid to spend that much on shoes." To her that's a logical response. And if you say your car broke down beyond repair, she might say, "Well, it *is* old." This is actually a clumsy attempt at making you feel better, i.e. the car served its purpose for a long time and you are lucky for it.

But much of the time, it boils down to this: she is too sensitive and cannot handle emotional situations and upsets the way you have been led to believe that women should. Like our male counterparts, we get riled up by emotional outbursts or demonstrations. She may have so much empathy that it's intrusive for her psyche to take on someone else's emotional baggage, especially if, in her eyes, it's trivial stuff. Or she may trivialize something in order to dismiss it and thereby avoid upset.

During a fight, she may have said something highly inappropriate and, well, bitchy. When we're overloaded emotionally or physically, we may say and do things we don't mean, not to be cruel or play games, we're just trying to nip an unpleasant experience in the bud and doing a botched job of it. And if it gets to be too much, she may completely shut down, and selective mutism—the temporary inability to speak—may kick in. (We'll talk more about that in Chapter 17, on depression.)

There's also "alexithymia," the inability to identify what one is feeling and therefore, not being able to express it or describe it in words. If you tell her something that upsets her, she might not know it at first, or know why, so she might say, "Okay," when in actuality, she doesn't really feel okay about what was just told to or asked of her. This can make for some sticky wickets and seeming contradictions. We have a reputation for "saying what we mean and meaning what we say," but if we don't know what we are feeling at the time, we can't. If you've just asked her to go somewhere that you know contains a lot of things that will overload her and she meekly says "sure," she probably doesn't really want to, she just isn't aware of all the feelings that just coursed through her veins in reaction to the question. A meek and quiet response is a clue that she's conflicted. Talk it through and make the right decision with open eyes. Even older Aspies like myself have alexithymia. I know I'm feeling something, just not sure what or why, and that is one of the biggest causes of conflicts in my relationships.

At the same time, she has an animal intuition that can be a little spooky and seem unfounded to others. In my experience, people on the spectrum seem to possess a sort of sixth sense when it comes to emotions. Just like the flicker of a fluorescent light that an NT can't see, she'll pick up on things that you (or others) are not outwardly telling her or showing her. While you might be smiling at her on the outside, telling her everything is fine, she might melt down or shut down, knowing somehow that something else is going on underneath. The worse thing to do is say, "You're imagining it." When someone tells us we are imagining something that we are sure we are feeling, it makes us either defensive or mistrustful of whoever's saying it, so do be tactful. If you are the person in question, examine your feelings and be honest with her. Tell her what's going on. If it is a third party, e.g. a friend, waiter, etc., say instead that perhaps it might be possible, but perhaps unproductive, to go with that assumption. People show us what they want for a reason.

For her, being in an emotional situation can be scary—like being trapped in a pen with an untamed horse, one which is clearly stronger and more volatile than she is. But emotions too can be tamed, and I know of no better way than through discussion, awareness, and possibly some sort of mind–body integration exercises like yoga. Sweeping things under rugs means that the carpet's going to get bumpy and sooner or later, someone's going to trip. It's better to face things as they come up, in a rational, supportive, nonjudgmental manner—this goes for both of you. Learn to broach subjects in a way that doesn't upset her or get her defenses up. If you are angry, wait until you've cooled down so that you are acting not reacting. It isn't just Aspies who have alexithymia; many people don't know what they're feeling half the time, or if they do, they don't know why. Some reading, possibly therapy, and plenty of good mindful conversation will do wonders for helping her to express things like joy, sadness, anger, in an appropriate manner. And nothing beats unconditional love.

If something is important to you and you need her to express empathy, it's helpful to give a firm, gentle reminder of that. You will probably have to do that much more than once, over the course of your lives together. Again, our lack of theory of mind means that we can place other people's passions and feelings into the low-priority pile. If your treasured grandma has just died, her response should definitely be more supportive than "Well, she *was* 94." If you miss your friends because your relationship has taken over all your spare time, her reaction should be more delicate than "They're losers anyway." Tact is the giftwrap on the package that makes us want to open it, and she must learn to wrap her words just a little bit, for the sake of your affection for one another.

It is not just in fights or arguments that feelings might reach an uncomfortable level. Some of us don't like to say or hear "I love you." As much as she may care for you and want to know it is reciprocated, the words still might make her squirm and feel uncomfortable once uttered. Equally, public demonstrations of affection might make her feel embarrassed and exposed. Asking permission before grabbing her for a streetside smooch is probably advisable.

Most of us express ourselves much better through the written word, or art, or music, when dealing with emotion. If you and she can write to each other, via email or text, or perhaps keep journal entries that you then let the other read, you might see that you are both much more sensitive and wise than face-to-face conversation between you reveals. The best advice I can give you is not to jump to conclusions where her feelings are concerned, because she speaks a slightly different language and some things might get lost in literal translation. But you do deserve to know that your partner loves you, so explain that to her—that sometimes even NTs need things spelled out.

PARTNER'S WORDS

"Because I expect her to mean what she says, I do get blindsided when she doesn't know what she's feeling so therefore cannot tell me. Working on communication together, is an ongoing process, she has to learn to identify her feelings and work on not saying 'Yes' when she means 'No.' It's been getting better, slowly but surely. Working on these issues has brought us closer together than I've ever felt with anyone else."

17

Depression—the enemy on our borders

Nobody gets down like an Aspie. Your Aspergirl may have phases where she lies on the couch for days, exhausted, wallowing in junk food, pajamas, sad thoughts, and tragic films. This is not just "downtime" which should itself take no more than a day. If, three days later, she's still as motivated as a sloth, we're talking depression.

There are various causes, but I believe that depression is usually linked to a loss or a feeling of powerlessness. Think about it: money, love, career, social failures, even death of a loved one—are all examples of how we feel powerless to have the thing we need to be happy. A broken love affair, a bad exam grade, being treated rudely by peers, these things can all contribute. Everyone deals with these things. Neurotypicals seem to be able to put setbacks into perspective better than we can, or handle more of them. But we have a much harder time, hence the need for downtime every time we throw ourselves into the world. But if too many things go wrong, or if we simply become overloaded and exhausted, it morphs into depression right before your very eyes, and before you know it, you open your bedroom door to find a pair of red eyes peering out at you from under a blanket in a darkened room. It is so hard to face people when you feel like this. Aspies who go to work in offices every day should get purple hearts for bravery, or lifetime achievement awards from the Academy, for they are the best actors in the world.

I do believe that exercise, nutrition/good health and LOVE have a lot to do with our capacity for joy. So how can you, the partner, help the situation? Well, if you are going to shunt her off to a doctor, try a nutritionist who specializes in autism spectrum conditions first. If you are thinking about a therapist, a CBT or person-centered counselor (cognitive behavioral and talk therapy, respectively) would be a safer first stop than a psychiatrist with a ready prescription pen. She may be on meds, and they may be quite helpful. But I am not a big believer in using meds to correct brain chemistry, until the day someone can tell me exactly what all of those brain chemicals are and exactly what measurements of each are needed to be happy. (I'm not saying never take meds, I'm just saying use them wisely. Even so-called benign meds like Prozac have had a litany of sometimes serious side effects. See the resources section for a link to a watchdog site that shows prescription drugs and side effects.)

Do the two of you have a physically healthy relationship? If it consists of mostly TV watching and eating, I'd say maybe not. Ever go hiking together, skating, rock climbing, anything physically fun and interesting? If not, make the change. Get outdoors together.

Are you in love and getting along? Whether or not you are part of the problem, please don't take an "Oh, she's just depressed" attitude. Those who take the lazy or apathetic approach can regret it later if depression becomes chronic, or turns to suicidal thoughts and self-harm. Self-harm, such as cutting and bulimia, can be a person's way of venting their hurt and pain in a sort of simulated suicide. Particularly something that leaves marks and scars—talk about a cry for help!

Never ignore depression. If your Aspergirl is depressed but is truly coping in a constructive way (for example, she's seeing a counselor, working out, and eating well) and says, "I'm working it out, leave me alone so I can do so," then it's probably alright to. But in so many relationships men in particular don't feel that it's their job to attend to someone else's emotional well-being. Rubbish, I say. We are all human beings who should express love and care for our loved ones. You should never become a punching bag or dumping ground for another, but we are all caretakers to some extent to our significant other, whether it's administering band-aids, cups of tea, an ear, some advice, or something even more extreme. If you want to see an exemplary proactive male, watch the documentary movie *The Horse Boy* about a father who takes his autistic child to Mongolia to see the horses... and a shaman. You'll be amazed at the story, particularly the ending. If he'd left the nurturing to his wife, she would not have come up with the same plan as he. A plan that literally worked miracles.

In a rage meltdown, she'll probably say too much; in depression mode, not enough. She may even have selective mutism while down. Selective mutism, which I mentioned in Chapter 16, is the temporary inability to speak. This is more than just being quiet, it is more like a seizure, and it physically hurts when this happens, especially when we are younger. Imagine having a golf ball stuck in your throat— pleasant, huh? Now at the same time, play a recording of self-loathing statements. You get the picture. This is the hell that is selective mutism. Nothing cures it but time alone or with a nonjudgmental friend.

Sometimes the depression is so all-consuming we practically become catatonic. I confess I recently went through one of these horrific phases, to my surprise because it had been happening less and less. A triple whammy of legal, financial, and personal problems all converged, each one a heavy burden in itself, but together more than I could bear. I barely spoke a word for an entire week, and it hurt all over. When this happens, I feel ashamed, I don't want to be seen, and will go days eating junk food and leaving my house as little as possible. If I didn't have dogs that count on me, if I didn't have other people with Asperger's looking up to me, I might not have had the strength to get up. If I didn't have a partner who looked at his role in it and made an honest effort to improve our relationship, I might still be there. It is the love we have for others, as well as their love for us, that is the sweetest motivator.

If meltdowns are happening frequently, look for the cause. Sometimes it takes a little detective work to figure it out. Did she take too much sleep aid? Whether it's melatonin or clonazepam, too much can cause her body and spirits to drag the next day. Did you have a fight? Was it her fault? Was it yours? Chances are it was both of you, so do your part and apologize. (And don't say, "You first.") Make amends. New relationships are difficult for us. I had a lot more depression when I first moved in with my partner— new home, new surroundings, new routine, new dog, new friends, new restaurants, having to find things you both like to watch/do/listen to. Perhaps she is adjusting. Has something changed lately? Are either of you drinking more? Spending too much or not enough time with each other? New baby?

That aside, is she satisfied with her life: family, house, appearance, relationship, career, self-expression? Those items might need tackling. The modern search for Happiness through material possessions has landed us firmly in ennui. Sometimes doing good works for other people is a fantastic way to shake off doldrums. Perhaps the two of you could turn your attentions to helping others, either on the spectrum or some other population. I recently took part in a charity gig, raising money for orphans. I provided the entertainment. It was so much fun and so rewarding to focus on helping others.

One thing is for certain. Chronic depression can wreak havoc on a body and a family. She needs help, maybe in the form of therapy. Taking care of food and other physical/ emotional needs until she is up and about again should speed the process. Criticism will only make it last and last.

"You're such a baby. You have kids to take care of. What kind of woman wallows all day in tears watching kids' movies? What's wrong with you? If you don't snap out of it I'm going to my mom's. I'll be at the pub." All not good things to say. Any of it sound familiar? If so, change your tactics and your mindset.

Depression is the shadow side of Asperger's and a sister to anxiety, an enemy on our borders, and we have to stay vigilant against it. It is why so many of us were misdiagnosed as borderline, or manic depressive. It is one of those things that needs multiple remedies and strategies, always on hand, to repel it. On a positive note, it can inform creativity once it has dissipated, and can also create a more compassionate person. No one truly understands suffering unless they have suffered.

PARTNER'S WORDS

"When depression rears its ugly head, try to remember what your partner's triggers are and keep them away—whether it be a loud TV/talking, harsh odors (cooking or cologne, etc.). Know what her soothing mechanisms are and have them on hand: chamomile tea, low lights, heavy blankets, etc. Try not to argue, no matter how wrong she is or uncomfortable she makes you feel. You can write thoughts and questions down and address them later, as soon as the storm subsides, when she is receptive again. For in depression, or meltdown, she will not hear you. When the time is right, try to figure out the cause of the episode."

"I hold her tightly from behind, for as many minutes as necessary. It seems to make her feel better."

18

The mood swings...
do more than duck

If you have been with your girl for a while, you may have witnessed a thing called a meltdown. Meltdown is what happens when a spectrum person is overloaded, and at the end of her tether, all the tension and upset comes bursting out of her like an F-class tornado. And like tornadoes, this can range between a gale force and downright destructive. Meltdowns are similar to what a wailing child in a store is going through, but while that is merely awkward for parents and uncomfortabe for other shoppers, an autistic woman having a rage meltdown is an embarrassment to herself, is difficult for others to understand (what kind of grown woman acts that way?), and can even land herself in trouble. In my house, in the past, plates have been dashed and there was no Big Fat Greek Wedding going on at the time—rather it was a Big Fat Geek Venting. And while we can romanticize that we resemble Elizabeth Taylor in *Who's Afraid of Virginia Woolf?*, there's nothing romantic about it. Her logical age may be more mature (book smarts), but emotionally she may lag behind her chronological age.

No one should ever be someone else's punching bag, and while she probably has never gone at you, she may have smashed a vase or two in her life during one of these infamous autistic storms. Fear not, for the brain is a flexible organ, ever learning, ever growing, and even old Aspies learn new tricks. It is a combination of self-discipline and learning to value the things she and you own, as well as valuing your relationship. Since most meltdowns happen over sensory and social overload issues, by now you will have learned many techniques for avoiding meltdown, and spotting the signs of possible imminent threat. And of course, not all Aspies do have rage meltdowns. Some of us are quite calm most of the time.

Other than sensory and social overload, there may have been another trigger, a fight perhaps, over something relatively small that escalated, or perhaps something larger. But whether you committed a minor faux pas or a major one, violence is not acceptable. Don't yell at her, don't get physical, for that will only cause an escalation. Hold contact with her with your eyes and speak calmly, don't raise the volume or pitch of your voice, be firm and with a concerned tone, ask her to please wait a minute, and talk to you once she's able because she may hurt herself, you, or something she might later miss.

Rage meltdowns can happen in stores, at clubs, on the street, in your house (or someone else's), usually after some sensory overload and social letdown. If you were the cause of it or not, you'd best not pressure her to talk until she's ready. "I can't talk now" means *can't* not *won't*.

Once the meltdown is long over, then is the time to talk about it. Not during. During, she will be almost unreachable. When I'm in meltdown mode, I can neither see nor hear clearly, and afterwards often cannot believe what I said or did. Later, you can ask her what more both of you can do to spot the signs. And while punitive measures are not as good as prevention, she needs to know that that sort of behavior is destructive to any relationship and that violence will not be tolerated.

After a rage meltdown, the recovery should be about a day. Avoid letting it turn into depression, by taking care of her, talking about what set it off and being sympathetic to whatever that was, easier of course if you were not the cause of it.

Some of us have learned to allow our anger to turn into tears. While this shows our vulnerability, and she doesn't want to be thought of as weak or bipolar, she can't get arrested for crying so this is preferable. Physical exercise such as running is handy, but when a meltdown hits, we don't exactly have the wherewithal to hit the gym. Still, having a kickbag in the garage couldn't hurt.

Look for the cause and address it. Don't be too quick to drag your girl to the shrink and to blame her for being unhinged. That's what my husband did, and the jaded, overworked, tunnel-visioned academic in a white coat looked down his Ivy League nose at me and started prescribing lots and lots of meds that landed me on a quick, slippery slide into a mental institution. That husband is long gone, I'm happy to say. My new partner talks to me, and helps me try to figure it all out. He lets me know he's not judging me.

Constant meltdowns and mood swings take their toll on the body's health. If you've both tried absolutely everything and are still riding that rollercoaster a little too often, research the best mood stabilizers for autistics. According to some autism experts, we can be very sensitive to drugs and can sometimes have the opposite reaction to a drug than expected. Don't assume a doctor knows all this. They have many patients. You have only one: Her. Use the internet to research. I've included a link in the resources section to a site that contains reports of side effects. With medication, as Temple always says, the benefits should outweigh the risks.

Speaking of being sensitive to drugs, recreational use should be pretty much verboten and alcohol should be consumed in moderation, if at all. Even neurotypicals have rage meltdowns from drinking, so why shouldn't it open the flood gates for the Aspie?

Please don't accuse her of concocting some elaborate scheme to have her way when she has a meltdown. It is way beyond that. Needing to have our way, as we discussed, is a deep-seated need that has no superficial or cheap motivations.

PARTNER'S WORDS

"If a meltdown is potentially on the way, don't be loud or combative, don't play loud music, get her in a quiet place. Offer her whatever her soothing mechanisms are. She's thrown stuff at me. I'm not a punching bag, but I didn't hold a grudge. At first I didn't understand but I forgave because I have somebody in my life who's able to explain what a meltdown is. That's important, especially if you're an NT, you need somebody to explain what it is and what they need. Talk about it before it happens so you can be prepared if and when it does."

19

Trust—abuse it and lose it

I was taking my dog out and the neighbor was taking hers. As we bumped into each other in the hallway, she said, "We should take our dogs out for a play date sometime." I kind of grunted some response and afterward said to my partner, "I don't think I want to go on a play date with her. I don't even know her." My partner told me not to worry, he said that NTs don't always mean what they say. "Then why would you bother saying it?" I asked.

That is the exact kind of situation that got me into so much trouble as a young adult. Someone would say, "Let's hang out." And I'd call them and call them until I either got them to hang out with me or admit that they didn't want to. NTs seem to have a way of saying things they don't mean and meaning things they don't say. There's been so much talk in this book about what is unusual or challenging about your Aspergirl, what she needs to learn, how you can help your "normal" friends understand her. Tell me, why is that kind of behavior considered acceptable?

The longer I live, the more I think that what's normal is due for review and revision. In a culture that prizes competition over cooperation, that rewards people for being devious and deceitful, that drops bombs instead of food, that shoots real bullets instead of something that just stuns someone long enough to stop them, that gives bimbos and bimbobs their own TV shows just to make everyone else feel superior and titillated at the same time, maybe we should rethink what normal is.

When an Aspie says, "I don't remember," they mean "I don't remember," not "I have no recollection of that at this juncture." Your Aspergirl is a straight-up player and will expect the same from you. She says what she means and means what she says and expects the same of you. If she sees, over the course of time, that you do not operate along these lines, she will think of you as flawed.

Everyone makes mistakes, you and she will too. But so much emphasis has been put on improving her, what about you? If you don't take my advice on at least most of these things, if you have been judgmental of her and keep on being judgmental, then eventually you won't have to give up on her, she will give up on you.

You must be honest. This is not on the optional menu. Things leave an indelible mark on our minds. An NT woman *might* be able to pretend that an affair, slight, or lie didn't happen, but your Aspie won't be able to. She might not remember where you parked the car, and she might not remember what that fight was about last night, but once something happens that kills her trust for you, it will be very difficult ever to get it back. Betrayal, particularly deceit, cheating etc., will leave an irreparable tear in the fabric of your relationship.

Betrayal doesn't have to be of the obvious sort either. If she begins to think that you really don't "get" her, that you really are not on her side, that will likely be the beginning of the end. If you find you are at this stage in your relationship, you will have to take strong proactive steps to regain that trust. Actions speak louder than words, but it would be helpful to write down what it is you intend to do (or not do) and then make sure your actions follow suit.

PARTNER'S WORDS

"Trust is a difficult thing to obtain, and keep, once you have it from your Aspie partner. Due to the many years of being bullied and being misunderstood, the 'Glass Wall' is tough to break down. Be patient. Be honest. Be supportive. Your Aspie partner will appreciate your efforts and not soon forget them."

20

Is it obsession or is it love?

I've heard NTs say that there are a million people in the world that would be compatible for each of us, but I do think the playing field is a lot narrower for Aspies. Even the most physically attractive of us tend to weed out most potential partners the moment we open our mouths, because we "say the wrong thing" or expose that we are quirky and not within the norms with either language or action.

In school most of us had a hard time dating. Like Groucho Marx said, "I'd never want to belong to a club that would have me as a member." The only boys that wanted to go out with us tended to be the ones we didn't want, because even us geeky kids want to go out with the cool kids to get accepted into that club; to be validated as desirable. So we may have grown up thinking we would never meet anyone who we actually liked and who liked us.

The dating game, which seemed like fun for everyone else was probably daunting to her. So if and when someone made out he liked her, and she liked him, chances are that she would obsess—this person would have become her special interest. This means that when breakup time came, if the other person was the one to initiate it, she might have found it very hard to let go. She may have become extremely distraught, for what are we without our obsessions? To an Aspergirl it is like being a kite without a string, a boat without a rudder, a soul with no *raison d'être*. She may have even gone into stalking-type behavior. And of course, because we are female, the other person might not have the same desire to bring this to the attention of school or other authorities, so it may have gone on for ages. One boy in high school was so tired of me chasing him, he finally hit me in the leg with a shovel to get rid of me.

She may have suffered similar traumatic experiences being rejected and humiliated as a teenager or young woman, and she might be gun-shy of any relationship at all. But others are virtually incurable romantics, despite the hurt it can bring. Of those, most of us eventually learn to curtail romantic obsessive behavior, but it can take a while. She is trusting, naïve and becomes obsessive about things she likes. Don't play games, even if they're the games everyone else in the world plays. Even if she's very high-functioning and doesn't miss all hints, she'll still miss some, and because we always want so desperately to believe that the one we love loves us back, nowhere is she more likely to fall into this trap.

Until recently, I had spent my whole life in a pattern of obsess, pursue, and eventually be rejected. What happens between pursuit and rejection is the only varying part. Sometimes I'd win the object of my affection for a short time. I can be quite persuasive, and men will be men and boys will be boys and I mistook sex for love. I was usually the "interim girl," you know, the one you have while you're looking for the One: a normal girl, that talks about normal things, that doesn't act weird; the one you want to be seen with. My own "great love" was really a one-sided obsession that lasted seven years although the actual relationship dragged out over three, and much of that was filled with lonely, sleepless, tearful nights, because he was never committed. This is when you'll hear people say, "How can a smart girl be so stupid?" or some variation on that theme.

When I interviewed couples for this book, some of the partners were exes. It became obvious in some cases that they broke up because they just couldn't handle Aspie quirks, and saw them as flaws rather than as things to be celebrated. This may be the case in your relationship. If you don't love her just as she is, if you don't see a future with her, if you don't want to go out with her, say so very specifically.

Ignoring her as a way of breaking up with her won't work as she probably won't get it. The be literal rule—"Say what you mean and mean what you say" totally applies here. She might be the last to know. Don't blindside her. Have discussions and help her prepare. It won't be easy. If she loves you or is obsessed with you, and you want to leave her, you will have to be both compassionate and firm, or it can drag on forever.

If you are worried about what will happen to her when you go, let me say this. She might be better off without you if you don't embrace her and her Aspie nature wholeheartedly. I have heard from couples that were flying blind for years, not knowing that she had Asperger's, until they finally broke up. Divorce and a diagnosis can give a woman a real understanding of herself and a real sense of freedom to do what she wants and to be who she really is. A dysfunctional home is not better than an unconventional home. Your kids, if you have them, would rather see two happy parents than two unhappy ones, even if that means in two separate places. Maybe not at first, but in the long run.

Just because she has Asperger's, doesn't mean you don't have issues of your own to work on. Be sure that if you do want to leave, you aren't needlessly blaming Asperger's for things that are actually within you. This can and does happen.

If you do love her, say so and say so often, even if it makes her squirm. Make it clear how you feel about her, and she in turn will make it clear how she feels about you (even if she doesn't verbalize it herself). If you want to stay together, you must completely embrace Asperger's and all it has to offer, and help your partner and yourself meet the challenges with patience, grace, information, and tools. It can be done. After several failed marriages and relationships,

I have someone who gets it and who works with me, from where I truly am, not from who or where he thinks I should be. That has made all the difference.

HER WORDS

"In a nutshell, after 22 years of marriage, out of the blue (to me anyway—I was totally clueless and blindsided!), he served me with divorce papers. Two weeks later, I had a formal diagnosis. I'll skip over all the drama that ensued, but know that I have never been happier. The divorce removed such a dark cloud that had been over me for probably decades, that I never even realized was there—my friends and family all commented how much I have blossomed and how much happier I seem. My own feelings are that removing a totally dysfunctional home situation, coupled with me embracing my Aspie nature and finally having insight into myself, all combined to bring about this transformation."

21

You may find more in
common as you get older

If you and your Aspergirl stay together into old age, you may find yourselves "trading traits." She may become less sensitive to things like loud noises and smells, and you might find yourself becoming more "Aspie" with age: more forgetful, perhaps a bit more blunt, disliking crowds, surprises, and really needing your ritual and routine. Even before old age, ask any neurotypical who's lived with an Aspie for a long time, and they'll tell you they've picked up a habit or two. As time goes by you might be more similar than complementary—two as-peas in a pod. That is something to look forward to.

I love getting older. I feel more comfortable in my skin, I've acquired some social skills, am less afraid of people, and actually do enjoy their company from time to time. I have learned to love my honesty while at the same time curbing my bluntness just enough. I've learned to embrace, use, and make a living off of my special interests, and I've become less self-centered through the love I have for my daughter. And your Aspergirl too will become more at peace with herself while learning to compromise, as long as you have good communication, acknowledgment of the impact of AS (on everything), and support. Support can be a therapist, group, family, books like this, or just the love of one good person.

But if I hadn't gotten a diagnosis, I'd hate to think about what my life would be like now, much less in my seventies. Golden years would not be golden, but rather a dingy yellow. I still have time to work on my challenges, my deficits, my relationship skills. Before we are too old to change, this is the time of life we need to come to terms with ourselves, our choices, our past, and where we are now in order to move happily into our futures. If your girl is in, say, her forties, she may be more accepting of herself, but you may have noticed some traits getting worse as she enters the middle years.

She may have gotten a late diagnosis because of it, or you may be going through a rough patch. As we enter into various menopausal states, we may become more emotionally unstable than we've been since puberty. In our twenties, thirties, and probably early forties we can "muscle" through, persevere, and when we encounter problems, consult counselors, gurus, psychics, and even tarot cards for the reasons we just can't seem to make relationships/career/ friendships work. But by the time we are mid-forties, give or take, we start to realize there's something more going on. As Liane Holiday Willey famously coined, we have a harder time "pretending to be normal." When I just turned 40, I was on my way to a class and suddenly could not remember where I was going. I had to pull over and just relax, allow it to come back to my brain. It took several minutes, and I thought I was suffering early Alzheimer's.

In middle age, Aspie traits we managed to bury through artifice and Herculean effort rise to the surface like Mafia victims washing up on a beach. It gets harder to put up with the social artifice and sensory overload of life. So we don't. We speak our minds about it. The trick is to do it nicely. I think this will be a crucial phase of your relationship because you may not like the newly liberated Maude as much as she likes herself. But Asperger's + maturity can mean one hell of an interesting person. Since my diagnosis, I started doing standup comedy, singing jazz professionally, and I've almost completed my sixth book (including this one), all within just a few years. If she is changing things, going through a rebuilding process, it is likely that the structures that are failing her were due a revision anyway. And though things like sleeplessness and forgetfulness may worsen, we have an edge—the childlike qualities inherent in autism and Asperger's keep us youthful and growing in many ways.

You will get older too, and AS or not, you will begin to suffer the same cognitive glitches that we do: "Where do I know you from?" "Who moved the supermarket?" You will become less coordinated with age, and as your eyes change, more sensitive to light and glare, while her hearing may decrease, making her less sensitive to sounds that currently drive her up a wall. In some ways, although people on the spectrum retain childlike qualities, we are also like older people in that we can be "fuddy duddies" not wanting to try new things. My point is, you may find more in common as you get older. Many older people, spectrum or not, are described as eccentric. It's because they've climbed the mountain of life and figured out what is important to them and what isn't and aren't afraid to express it. She's already been there for ages, saying come on up, the view is great!

PARTNER'S WORDS

"She doesn't let me be in denial. She forces me to see things from a different perspective...which can get pretty uncomfortable at times, but I've changed and grown so much because of her."

"I've been the female partner of an Aspergirl for ten years. It's complicated and difficult sometimes... We don't think in the same way or see things the same way. As time goes by, we both learn to accept each other for who we are... I wouldn't change a thing!"

22

Asperger's is a reason,
not a label, not an excuse

What good is a label, I often get asked? Doesn't it pigeonhole a person? Prejudice others against you? Well, you can't be responsible if other people are prejudiced. Generally, in modern societies we don't ask other minorities to hide who and what they are (anymore). We are what we are, whether we hide it or not.

My advice is, diagnosed or self-diagnosed, if the information describing Asperger's describes her and the advice given to people on the spectrum helps her, then use it. Whether you share that outside of your relationship is up to the two of you. But since you are the most intimate person in her life, you have to know what you are dealing with. Knowing about AS will help you know her and, in turn, inform and enrich your relationship. All my prior relationships existed outside of that knowledge. I can only tell you that knowing, and having a partner that knows, is so completely different to anything I've experienced before. For the first time, I am not alone in a relationship.

Your Aspergirl may be 20 or she may be 40. If she is younger and has good parents and can find a good doctor, she might get an actual formal diagnosis. I've been compiling a list of doctors that diagnose adult females and it is longer than your arm…if you're a dachshund. So if she cannot find someone, or if she cannot afford it, she may be self-diagnosed. That is okay. That is how most of us start out. I talk to women all the time that have been self-diagnosed for years and are just getting their official verdict now. Sometimes, rarely, they come back and say the doctor did not agree with their own assessment, but often they do.

My advice is, if she's self-diagnosed, accept it. If the information helps her, what harm could it possibly do? Most people I meet, do NOT use Asperger's as an excuse but rather as an explanation. It explains our bluntness, will to perfection, our childlike qualities, meltdowns, our rigidity, our focus, our strange sense of humor that serves a lot better than it receives. It explains so many things. But before you go pinning a big scarlet "A" onto everything she says and does, and onto every problem with your relationship, remember that she is a person, and yours is a relationship, and you are playing the other leading role. You may have your own issues to learn about and get ahold of.

Don't ever think that a diagnosis means she is fatally flawed, or that she can now be "cured." Neither is correct, and that kind of thinking would be the death of your relationship. But she should be getting help and knowledge, at least in the form of books and dialogue, if not therapy or AS groups. She still has few resources to turn to, since all work on AS was done observing men, and not until very recently (and I like to think I had a small part in it) has it begun to be understood that AS presents and is perceived differently in women, before which it had been overlooked if not misdiagnosed. She's a minority within a minority, and again if she's an ethnic minority or gay. The shortlist of authors, speakers, and researchers who deal positively and deeply with female AS issues is indeed still a short list. Other than myself, Liane Holiday Willey, Shana Nichols and Tony Attwood are the first that spring to mind (please forgive those I missed). All of them really get it and really care, Liane because she's a beautiful compassionate author who is on the spectrum, and Shana and Tony because they work intensely and mindfully with Aspergirls at their clinics and have written great books.

So other than reading our books, and maybe getting a diagnosis, where can she turn? Why should she turn? Because she is from a different subculture and needs to understand who she is. I wouldn't want to be an African girl for example, in an all-white neighborhood without ever seeing anyone of my own color. I'd always feel different, no matter how kind everyone was to me. It's a human need to belong, to know why you are different from those around you, and to seek out others like us, even for Aspies. I never feel more comfortable than when I speak in a roomful of spectrum individuals. I love giving talks to professionals who work with us, but am more fulfilled and challenged by talking with fellow Aspergians. She probably has this need even if you both think she doesn't. You might want to seek out any Asperger adult social/support groups in your area.

There's maybe a stigma in your mind attached to these groups. Every time I've gone to one there has always been an interesting cross-section of men and women of different ages, with different interests, aptitudes, and styles: *Individuals.* Should you attend these groups with her? Of course, if they'll have you (most will, although a few have a strict AS-only policy). She spends most of her time in an NT-dominated world, why shouldn't you see how the other 1 percent lives? It is a beautiful, rich world we inhabit.

A diagnosis will give both of you a much-needed frame of reference for many of the challenges and differences between you that you will encounter. I hope that this book has given you understanding of your exotic, eccentric, unique Aspergirl. And I thank you for caring and for spending a few hours of your life with this handbook.

PARTNER'S WORDS

"I didn't believe she had Asperger's until I got to know her. But if I didn't have an understanding, if I hadn't educated myself, I wouldn't have understood so many things about her. I sometimes think that learning about Asperger's has enriched me more than it has her, made me wiser and more compassionate. I wouldn't change a thing."

LAST WORDS

As I went for a walk and wondered how to end this book, the words to a song popped into my head over and over again. "Are you strong enough to be my man?" Women with Asperger's are not looking for some malleable, weak-willed person they can manipulate into giving them everything they want. We are looking for someone who is strong enough to handle the challenges we'll throw his way, but who can also challenge us. But even the bravest adventurer can be confounded by unfamiliar terrain, and climate conditions they are not prepared for. Real love and companionship are treasures. I don't want you to give up on the hunt because you don't have a map. Now you have one. Good luck to you both!

GLOSSARY OF TERMS

Alexithymia: difficulty in experiencing, expressing, and describing emotional responses (http://dictionary.reference.com/browse/alexithymia).

Asperger's syndrome (AS): an autism spectrum condition first described by Hans Asperger. It is a milder form of autism, characterized by qualitative impairment in social interaction. This is manifest through impairment in nonverbal behaviors, e.g. eye contact, facial expression, body postures and gestures; failure to develop appropriate peer relationships; lack of social reciprocity; restricted, repetitive patterns of behavior, interests, and activities; inflexible adherence to routines or rituals, and abnormal preoccupations.

It is now widely understand that many people on the autism spectrum possess strong focus and special talents, and in some cases, a level of genius in one or more areas.

Aspie: a person with Asperger's syndrome. Not derogatory, but an informal term which is popularly used in forums and self-reference.

Autism spectrum conditions (ASC): also known as *pervasive development disorders*. They are characterized by varying degrees of impairment in communication skills, social interactions, and restricted, repetitive, and stereotyped patterns of behavior. They can range from severe autism to Asperger's syndrome.

Executive function: "a set of cognitive abilities that control and regulate other abilities and behaviors" (www.minddisorders.com/Del-Fi/Executive-function.html).

Neoteny: a slowing of the rate of development with the consequent retention in adulthood of a feature or features that appeared in an earlier phase in the life cycle of ancestral individuals (e.g. neoteny in the ostrich has resulted in adult birds sporting the down feathers of nestlings) (http://dictionary.reference.com/browse/neoteny).

Neurotypical (NT): although not the strict definition, this is a term often used to describe a person who does not have Asperger's or any other autism spectrum condition.

Theory of mind: "the ability to attribute mental states—beliefs, intents, desires, pretending, knowledge, etc.—to oneself and others and to understand that others have beliefs, desires and intentions that are different from one's own" (Simon Baron-Cohen, cited at http://en.wikipedia.org/wiki/Theory_of_mind#Defining_theory_of_mind).

BIBLIOGRAPHY AND OTHER RESOURCES

BIBLIOGRAPHY

Attwood, S. (2008) *Making Sense of Sex: A Forthright Guide to Puberty, Sex and Relationships for People with Asperger's Syndrome.* London: Jessica Kingsley Publishers.

Attwood, T. (2006) *The Complete Guide to Asperger's Syndrome.* London: Jessica Kingsley Publishers.

Holliday Willey, L. (1999) *Pretending to Be Normal.* London: Jessica Kingsley Publishers.

Holliday Willey, L. (2011) *Safety Skills for Asperger Women: How to Save a Perfectly Good Female Life.* London: Jessica Kingsley Publishers.

Nichols, S. (2009) *Girls Growing Up on the Spectrum.* London: Jessica Kingsley Publishers.

Simone, R. (2009) *22 Things a Woman Must Know If She Loves a Man with Asperger's Syndrome.* London: Jessica Kingsley Publishers.

Simone, R. (2010a) *Asperger's on the Job: Must-Have Advice.* Arlington, TX: Future Horizons.

Simone, R. (2010b) *Aspergirls: Empowering Females with Asperger Syndrome.* London: Jessica Kingsley Publishers.

ONLINE RESOURCES

Ms. Simone's Asperger website
www.help4aspergers.com
For a list of female Asperger traits, diagnosing doctors, my calendar, and much more.

Ms. Simone's Fantasy trilogy featuring an Aspergian hero
www.OrsaththeFool.com

Comedy and jazz site
www.rudysimonecomedyjazz.com

Ms. Simone's personal Facebook page
www.facebook.com/profile.php?id=100000224576377
Look for Ms. Simone's books on Facebook as well!

Psychiatric Drug Side Effects Reported to the U.S. FDA
www.cchrint.org/psychdrugdangers/medwatch_psych_drug_adverse_
reactions.php

OTHER BOOKS BY RUDY SIMONE

The Fool—Part I: Orsath the Singer (2010).
The Fool—Part II: Orsath the Traveler (2011).